Whimsical Tarot

A DECK FOR CHILDREN AND
THE YOUNG AT HEART

Written by Dorothy Morrison

Illustrated by
Mary Hanson-Roberts

U.S. GAMES
SYSTEMS, INC

Published by
U.S. GAMES SYSTEMS, INC.
Stamford, CT 06902 USA

First Edition

Library of Congress Cataloging-in-Publication Data

Morrison, Dorothy, 1955-
    The whimsical tarot: a deck for children and the
    young at heart/ written by Dorothy Morrison;
    illustrated by Mary Hanson-Roberts.
        p. cm.
    Includes bibliographical references.
    ISBN 1-57281-315-6
    1.Tarot. 2. Fairy tales--Miscellanea. I. Title.

BF1879.T2 M69 2001
133.3'2424--dc21   2001033066

06 05 04 03 02 01
10 9 8 7 6 5 4 3 2 1

Printed in Canada

U.S. Games Systems, Inc.
179 Ludlow Street
Stamford, CT 06902 USA
www.usgamesinc.com

Dedication

To the Celtic Goddess, Rhiannon—the original Mother Goose—and to children the world over who ponder Her every word.

In Memory of...
A. J. Sargent—my dear friend and adopted father—who wanted this deck, pushed for this deck, and believed in my ability to create it.

Oscar, the little dog who, in his own way, brought this project into reality.

Acknowledgements
To Stuart Kaplan, who believed in this deck enough to take a second look and make my dreams come true.

To Mary Hanson-Roberts, who was able to look into my mind's eye and bring life to its visions with a wave of her magical brush.

To Gay Bost, Donna Sharley, Sandy Sargent, Pat Monaghan, Sirona Knight, and Trish Telesco, who offered the magic of love, friendship, and encouragement every step of the way.

Goddess bless you, every one!

Contents

Preface

As parents, we feed and clothe our children. We nurture and love them. We do their dirty laundry, make their beds, and help with their schoolwork. We teach them to be responsible adults. Sadly enough, though, we often skip the spiritual stuff; not because it isn't important, but because we think it's something they'll learn on their own. It's not.

We owe it to our children to give them a firm grasp of the Higher Self. They need to know that it's a real part of them— the part that reveals who they are, where they're going, and what they can accomplish. They need to know it holds answers that can ease their lives and bring about spiritual growth. It's important that they understand the wonders of that Self, and learn how to access its gifts. Our children can't do that, however, unless we provide them with the necessary tools. The Whimsical Tarot is such a tool.

Based on childhood images, the Whimsical Tarot provides a fresh approach to an old system. Because most children are already familiar with the imagery, they form an immediate connection to the cards. This enables them to free the Higher Self and get to know their spiritual side. They feed, nurture, love and care for it, and in return, the spiritual gifts once beyond their reach rain down upon them freely.

This system is designed to connect the ancient art of storytelling and spirituality. It involves reading to your children, telling them stories, and getting to know them as individuals. It takes careful planning and some time set aside from your busy day—time you could spend doing other things. Most of all, though, it takes love and understanding. However, if you take the time to help your children use this deck properly, The Whimsical Tarot will not only connect them to their most valuable asset, but may prove to be the most powerful parenting tool within your grasp.

Part One:

CHILDHOOD IMAGERY AND THE TAROT

Life is a whirlwind of images that leave an imprint upon the mind's eye. Some stay with us for a time and then fade away slowly. Others are much stronger. They make deep impressions and shine through in our personalities, affecting the way we handle everyday life. These are the images of the fairy tale and nursery rhyme. These are the images of childhood.

Why does this imagery pack such a wallop? What gives it so much impact? Let's take a quick look at the typical fairy tale outline and find out. There are good guys and bad guys. The good guys cheerfully endure some sort of aggravation, but in return, something wonderful always happens to them. They live happily ever after. The bad guys are terribly rotten. They plot and plan malicious mischief, but know matter how clever they are, they never win. Not ever.

We learn from this that crime doesn't pay, and that we get out of life exactly what we put into it. We not only learn that we must treat others well and keep our promises if we want to succeed, but that the struggles involved are always worthwhile and rewarded. These stories let us know that life is a fair exchange and regardless of the way things appear on the surface, our world is a safe place to live. Most important, though, they give us what today's world cannot. They give us hope.

In the adult world of responsibility and rat race, hope is a commodity often in short supply. It's little wonder, then, that we find the need to keep such images alive and well. We feed them. We nurture them. And when we're feeling down and out, we pull them out and play with them. Doing so allows us to go back in time, to a place that was happier, a place where the world was safe and fun, a place where cause and effect worked the way they were meant to, and where the villain always got his comeuppance.

Throughout our lives, we draw upon these childhood images for security and our personal sense of ethics. We use them as an escape from the stress of day to day living, and as examples of what is right and wrong with our world. They crop up in our dreams and fantasies. A part of every grown woman believes that Prince Charming will eventually sweep her up on his white horse and whisk her away to his castle. A part of every grown man longs to wake Sleeping Beauty with his kiss, or hear Rapunzel sing. Everyone wishes for a fairy godmother when things seem darkest, and no one can resist the promise of a pot of gold at the end of the rainbow.

Is this healthy? Yes. Even though our society places extreme emphasis on dealing with reality, we all need to see a ray of sunshine in our darkest moments. We need to know that good begets good, and bad begets punishment. It is a survival mechanism designed to keep us sane, teach us lessons and help us continue to put one foot in front of the other. For all practical purposes, this imagery allows the much needed temporary escape from the harshness of reality that enables us to live on a day to day basis.

How The Tarot Works

Childhood imagery provides excellent tools for working with the Tarot. Because these images already live in our subconscious, they provide a direct line from the mundane self to the spiritual self, and speed the response process.

For example, when you see Puss 'N Boots depicted as The Magician, you don't really have to read the card's definition to get a general idea of it's meaning. The image of Puss 'N Boots resurfaces clearly in the mind's eye, and you automatically remember how quick-witted, resourceful, and talented the cat was.

You remember how he took a rather grim situation and turned it around for his benefit. Looking at the card more closely, you'll see that he's a "take charge" kind of guy, and that he's in full control of the Elements and their powers. From this, the spiritual self concludes that The Magician card says you need to take charge of a situation and use what you know to solve it effectively. It says that you have the power to handle anything life deals to you, and in doing so, you have the ability to help yourself and others.

Why was that so easy? It is because our minds process thoughts as pictures, and the Whimsical Tarot is a system based on known imagery. When we see a symbol, the conscious mind (mundane self) tells the subconscious mind (inner child) to recall associated images. When these images form in the mind's eye, both sides of the spiritual self (the personal unconscious and the collective unconscious) awaken. The personal unconscious immediately processes all the knowledge, emotion, and imagery we've accumulated in our lifetime. At the same time, the collective unconscious sorts through our basic instincts and intuitive powers. They quickly bundle any data related to the images seen by the mind's eye or mundane eye, and send it directly back to the conscious and subconscious minds. Because the imagery and story of Puss 'N Boots already lives in each of the conscious, subconscious, and unconscious minds, the processing of information takes less time, and the card meaning is more quickly apparent.

This doesn't mean that you won't gain additional insight into The Magician and his message by reading the associated definition in this book. What it does mean is that you will have an immediate response to the card—an immediate feel for the card—and a head start on understanding its advice. This, in itself, will give a great deal of assistance in helping you or your child learn to read this deck.

Children? Read The Tarot?

Can children really be taught to read the Tarot? Absolutely. Perhaps one of the most common misconceptions about children is that they are childish folks with childish attitudes, and have little grasp of what's going on in the world around them. But, in order to teach children anything effectively, we have to get past that idea. We need to look at children with a fresh eye. We need to erase old beliefs and start anew by realizing that children are merely miniature people.

Sometimes we forget that a child's mind functions just as ours. Our old beliefs tell us that children come into this world without any knowledge at all. That simply isn't true. Yes, children learn by our example, but they also arrive with instincts, personality, and trust. Babies know when they're hungry. They know when they're safe. Most learn to crawl and walk all by themselves, and even if we didn't use repetitive phrases to teach them to talk, they'd eventually pick it up anyway.

A little quality time spent with your child will go a long way toward eradicating any of your old beliefs about children. I've discovered that my own child is more in tune with the workings of the universe than some of my friends, and he is capable of carrying on a much more intelligent conversation than most of them. According to the national averages, he isn't exceptionally smart. He isn't a child prodigy. He's just a child. A miniature person.

The greatest thing about children is that they are so open to world around them, and so eager to accept the unseen world of spirituality. As adults, we often have trouble with the latter, because over many years, we've become totally immersed in the expectations of society. We're afraid to accept what we feel, hear or see. Why? Because we worry that we might hear something that no one else does, or even worse, see something that is invisible to the rest of the world.

Being new to the world, children don't share these fears. They haven't been inundated by society; therefore, they haven't learned to stifle their creative spirituality. They listen to that which is seen and unseen, and hold it all in awe. They discount very little and miss nothing. When they come up with something that seems—by societal standards—ridiculous, everyone chalks it up to a vivid imagination. It's okay for a child's imagination to run wild. What's more, it's completely natural.

Because of their openness, unsullied perspectives, and potential creativity, children are excellent candidates for the art of card reading. And the younger they are, the better. What if they can't read words yet? No problem. What if they can't memorize? Forget it. You think they don't have a clear understanding of what's happening around them, or that they don't have the attention span for detail? Trust me, they do.

The fact is, anyone can read the Tarot. It doesn't take any special powers, clairvoyance, or psychic ability—though there certainly are people who develop those talents and use them to improve their reading skills. All it takes is a little imagination and the ability to follow a storyline. Much like the frames of a newspaper comic strip, the cards tell a story when they are put together in a layout.

This is why card reading comes so easily to children. They don't have to be able to read words—they only have to be able to speak them. Their psyches haven't been numbed like ours, and because children are still open to the magic in the world around them, the subliminal messages of the cards come through loud and clear. They pay close attention to detail, and being unafraid of judgment, they find it much easier to tap into their Higher Selves.

However, teaching children to tap into their own spirituality through card reading is just a small part of what this book is all about. It's about fertilizing their creativity, nurturing their imaginations, and keeping their magic alive and well. It's about forming that glorious bond between parent and child. The bond that is life itself. The bond that is magic incarnate.

The best way to create that bond and help your child grow spiritually and emotionally is to read aloud to him or her. My mother was—and still is—the best of storytellers. She set aside a special time in our household for reading; and for me, it was the best part of the day. I'd climb into her bed, prop myself up on what I thought were the most luxurious pillows in the world, and listen excitedly as Mama's voice unfolded each story.

One of the things that made that time so memorable, was that Mama had a very strong sense of the dramatic. She believed that no story was worth reading unless every character had a different voice and dialect. That practice gave each character his or her very own personality. It brought them to life and took me into their special worlds. Because of this, every story Mama read became an adventure with a life of its own. The characters lived and breathed, and Mama was the midwife.

Mama read to me until I was thirteen or so (that was about the time I became concerned about society's expectations of me and decided I was too grown up for that sort of thing). I learned a lot during those first thirteen years of life. I learned the difference between right and wrong. I discovered the fundamentals of cause and effect. What's more, I learned it in a fun and enjoyable fashion. The most important thing I learned, though, was that Mama loved me. Even when she was tired or didn't feel well, she always had time for me. And if she didn't, she *made* time. Through our daily reading time, she created a bond between us that's still stronger than any I've ever encountered. It made me feel safe and secure, and no matter what happened, I knew I could count on Mama.

That's why I think reading aloud to children is so important. There's no easier way to bond with them than to share yourself by daily reading. The sound of your voice becomes security and comfort. The story becomes the teacher, unfolding basic examples of getting along in the world. Time becomes a treasured gift. You, as the narrator, are suddenly the greatest gift of all; for by reading to your child, you become travel agent, magician, and friend.

The most precious thing that comes from reading time, though, is the gift of imagery. These images feed the inner child, develop creative energy, and keep personal magic alive and well. They shape who we can be, who we will be, and who, at last, we are. In short, they are necessary to the spiritual development of all humankind.

We've talked a lot about how shared reading time helps children. Now let's talk about what that time does for us as parents. Reacquainting ourselves with old childhood friends and recapturing their magic works like a good mental housecleaning. Simply put, it clears mind clutter. It sweeps the dust from our imaginations, and before we know it, our personal imagery sparkles again. We become more creative, more imaginative, and more at peace with our lives. Stress and worry are short-lived because we are able to solve problems more creatively. Best of all, our inner child breathes again, and when we allow that to happen, the joy of daily living resurfaces. We lose the need to be so serious, our sense of humor returns, and we are happier people. We owe that to ourselves. More importantly, we owe that to our children. Why? Because when we are happier people, they are, too.

What To Tell Your Child About The Tarot

Don't tell your child that reading cards is a way to predict the future. It's not. Contrary to popular belief, the Tarot doesn't work that way. It gives advice based on a current situation, a current set of circumstances, and a current path or choice.

Therefore, the outcome of a reading is subject to change if the path changes. It doesn't take much to change a path. For example, suppose a card reading advises that you are likely to

16

get a promotion and raise. Based on this, you decide not to go to work that day. You feel so confident, you don't feel the need to notify your boss. The next day, you go in expecting that raise and promotion, but get fired instead. What happened? By missing work and not calling in, you changed your path. Thus, you changed the circumstances that were current yesterday, and that card reading does not apply to the present ones. This is why some people feel cheated when the advice of a card reading doesn't come to pass.

Instead, explain to your child that the cards are a tool, and liken them to something they can understand. A rake is a good choice because it pulls the leaves away from the grass and exposes the lawn. A good rake works like the Tarot, for it uncovers that which is hidden beneath the surface and allows us to make decisions based on the total picture.

Deck Preparation

Many experts believe that a deck must be "prepared" or consecrated before the reader can use it effectively. They suggest that the reader sleep with the deck, carry it on their person, or shuffle the deck daily for a prescribed length of time so that the deck picks up the reader's vibrations. It has also been suggested that Tarot decks be wrapped in silk and housed in a special box. The list goes on and on.

The reason for these preparations has to do with the fact that the Tarot is not a game; rather, it is a sacred tool used to connect the world of spirituality with that of the mundane. In essence, it is used to contact the higher self for advice in dealing with situations we face in everyday life. Taking special steps to prepare a deck reinforces that idea in the conscious mind, and makes that part of us ready to accept any related information presented by the subconscious and unconscious minds.

While a certain amount of preparation may be good advice for adults, it seldom applies to children. Why? Because children possess a natural link to the spiritual world. They have very strong vibrations and "claiming" capabilities. They know when something belongs to them, and automatically infuse new items with their energies. They also instinctively know the difference between a toy and an item that is "special." For this reason, special deck preparation is unnecessary for children.

However, the inner child in all of us is especially fond of ritual. It likes playing dress-up, likes lighting candles, and feeling special. As the inner child plays an important role in the Tarot system, you might want to perform a mini-ritual to get its attention. Keep it short and simple, though, because the inner child doesn't have much patience. A sample ritual is included below for your convenience, but don't hesitate to make changes if it's not in keeping with your child's age or preference.

Tarot Deck Blessing Ritual

Materials:

>One white votive or birthday candle
>One cup of water
>Salt shaker, or a small amount of dirt or sand

Clear a small spot somewhere in the house that can be used for an altar space—even a windowsill will do. Help your child arrange the materials on the altar, then remove the cards from the box and place them there as well. Holding your child's hand, raise arms up toward the sky, and chant together:

>Lady of the Tarot, come out to play!
>Bless these cards, we ask and pray!

Have your child blow on the deck three times and say something like:

>I give you air to breathe!

Light the candle (if your child is very young, you may wish to handle the candle-lighting) and say:

>I give you light!

Sprinkle a few drops of water on the deck and say:

>I give you life!

Finally, sprinkle a few grains of salt or soil on the deck and say:

>I give you roots!

Ask your child to pick up the deck. Then join hands and thrust them skyward again. Say together:

>By Earth and Water, Fire and Air,
>
>These cards are blessed with loving care!

Thank the Lady of the Tarot (a simple "thank you" will do), and blow out the candle.

The Discovery Phase

After the ritual, let your child look through the cards. The discovery phase is important because the child infuses the deck with personal vibrations at this time and claims the deck as his or her own. Don't be concerned if your child seems to be playing with the deck or treating it much the same as his/her toys. In fact, the child may drag favorite toys into the room during this process. This is normal for some children. It's their way of introducing the cards to other "family members," and it is just a gesture of acceptance. Such behavior is also a sign that your child is having fun. This is good. As long as the cards are fun for your child, he/she will not lose interest in them.

More than likely, your child will become excited about particular cards, and invite you to look, too. Children all react differently during this phase. Some will offer cards to you, while others are more territorial and will only show them to you from a distance. Generally, though, card discovery opens itself to a very animated discussion with lots of questions and answers. It's a good idea to keep a notebook handy to jot down favorite cards and any interesting comments your child might make about them. These will be a great help when you teach your child to read.

Keep card reading simple, and make it fun. It's fine to make a game of it at first. The important thing is to get your child's attention. As children grow and learn, the realization of the Tarot's importance as a tool will, too.

The first step in reading the Tarot is to become familiar with the cards. Don't try to memorize the definitions in this book, and for now, don't look at the Tarot as a whole system. See it, instead, as several individual pictures that work together to make a complete set. This approach is less overwhelming.

Take one card from the deck and study it—without looking at the descriptions. Make a few notes. List your reaction to the card at first glance, then answer the following questions.

What are the occupants of the card doing? Study the expressions on their faces. Think about the related fairy tale, nursery rhyme, or song. What part did the characters play in the story? What do the colors say to you? How does the picture make you feel? Are you happy, sad, wary, or indifferent?

Close your eyes, and picture the card in your mind. When you're sure it's perfectly recreated there, open your eyes and take another look. What did you miss the first time? Symbols? Colors? Details? Write it all down. Then find the card in this book, and read about it to gain further information.

Now, give the card to your child, and ask a few simple questions. In the case of Temperance (a depiction of Jack and Jill), a the dialogue might go something like:

"What's going on in this picture?"

"The kids fell down and spilled their water."

"Why do you think that happened?"

"They were in a hurry."

You get the idea. Keep the conversation going for a while and take notes. Ask your child what else is happening in the picture. Does he or she like the card? Why or why not? Does it remind your child of someone? When the conversation winds down, recite the related nursery rhyme. This will grab the attention again, and afterward, things will probably be seen in the picture that weren't seen before. Share your findings with him or her, but keep it light and simple.

So what happens if your child isn't interested in that card? What if he or she pulls another from the deck instead? Stay calm, and don't worry. Discuss the new card, and make a note not to talk about the other one until a later time.

Pick two other cards, and follow the same procedure. Note the responses, then put all three cards together. Ask your child to make a story from the pictures—using the first card for the beginning, the second for the middle, and the third for the ending. Presto! Your child has just done his or her first reading.

No matter what happens, don't argue with your child over meanings. He or she may see or feel something that you don't. Remember that children have an excellent grasp of symbolism and live easily in both the worlds of the mundane and the spiritual. In fact, they often have trouble separating the two until society steps in and insists they learn how! They have an innate understanding of archetypes, too, and seem to embrace them more easily than we do. If you really feel your child is mistaken about a meaning, question rather than argue. Through a series of questions and answers, the child will easily see a mistake if there is one. On the other hand, the child's answers may serve to show you an angle you hadn't thought about.

Another excellent familiarizing technique is the visitation exercise, and nothing beats it for gaining new insight into the Tarot. That's because there's no other Tarot-related exercise that allows the reader to actually talk to the characters in the cards. No other exercise gives such an in-depth look into their personalities, or brings the reader close enough to the action to become a part of it. Use the instructions below to help your child, but don't discount using this exercise for yourself. You'll be amazed at what you discover about your own inner workings, and how the cards relate to you on a personal level.

Ask your child to pick a card and then to imagine that the card is growing. It gets bigger and bigger, wider and taller, until it fills the whole room. The characters in the picture spring to life. They move around. They talk to each other. They tend to whatever business is pictured in that card.

Tell your child that he or she can talk to the characters, and encourage that action. All the youngster has to do is take a mental step into the picture. Most children rush right in because their natural curiosity takes hold. If your child seems skittish, though, reassurance is in order. Take the child's hand, and say there's nothing to be afraid of. You are right there, and won't let anything bad happen. Explain that he or she can leave the picture whenever ready; then offer your accompaniment on the journey.

Once in the card, encourage your youngster to ask questions and get to know the characters. Have your child look around for things that went unnoticed before—under tables, behind chairs, along the seashore. If your child comes up with something not depicted in the card, don't be surprised. This is common. Allow your child to stay and play as long as he'd like.

When the child returns from the visit, ask questions. Find out what was asked, what was learned, and what was found. Were the characters nice? What did they say? Did the child find new objects in the card? Would it be fun to visit that place again some time? Why or why not?

Take careful notes and write everything down. They are a record of spiritual growth, and you'll want to refer to them later as your child's perception of the cards deepens.

Procedures, Layouts, and Other Good Stuff

Traditionally, card reading begins with the search for a significator. This is a card that represents the querent or person for whom the reading is being performed. However, you won't find that card included in any of the spreads listed below. For one thing, finding a proper significator can be a time-consuming process, as people change according to attitude, personality, and surrounding events. Secondly, children get bored if they have to spend time with too many preliminaries. Most importantly, though, is that the significator card really has no bearing on the reading. Its only purpose is to show the querent that he or she has a "personal card" present in the layout. This is unnecessary because the querent is not only present, but shuffles the cards and imbues them with personal energy before the reading begins.

The significator problem out of the way, let's start with the querent's question and a thorough shuffle. Concentrated focus on a question during the shuffle is important so that the advice obtained is appropriate to the inquiry at hand. Unless children are reading for someone else, they will be both the reader and the querent. Children are inquisitive by nature, so the question is seldom a problem. Card shuffling might present a dilemma, though, if your child hasn't perfected the technique. If this is the case, don't try to teach your child to shuffle right now. Doing so may cause feelings of inadequacy to surface and your child may lose interest. Instead, try one of the following methods.

Method 1:
Ask your child to spread the cards face down on a flat surface (the floor, a table, etc.) and mix them up with the fingers, just as if he or she were shuffling dominoes.

Method 2:
Have your child cut the deck into many small piles, then put them back together in any order.

Whatever technique you choose, ask your child to continue shuffling until he or she feels the deck is ready.

Choose a spread from the layout section, and position the cards according to the diagram. Have your child read the cards in the order they were placed. If some of the cards are upside down, ask the youngster to move them to an upright position.

So, what about the reversed meanings? Forget them. Like the significator card, they have no use in The Whimsical Tarot.

Why? Because neither the personal unconscious nor the collective unconscious responds well to reversals. When cards are reversed, both sides of the unconscious become confused. The flow of data to the conscious and subconscious slows down, and intuition seldom survives the process. This system is designed to eliminate those problems and still give accurate readings.

Layouts

For your convenience, the layouts are categorized according to age group. You may wish to choose a spread for younger children and let older ones decide for themselves. Don't be concerned if your child insists on using a spread designed for a younger or older age group. This may be just what the youngster needs to build self-confidence in his or her reading skills.

Ages 2 through 6
Layout 1: The One Card Spread

After shuffling the deck, choose one card. This may be any card—one turned up from the top of the deck, one turned up in a cut, or one pulled out from the middle. This spread is excellent for daily advice or for clarification of a specific problem.

Layout 2: The Three-Cut Spread

Shuffle the deck and cut it into three piles. Turn the piles face up, and read them left to right letting the pictures tell the story.

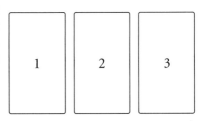

Ages 7 through 10
Layout 3: Yes/No Spread

This spread is helpful when a question can be answered with a simple yes or no. Shuffle the deck while concentrating on the question. Dealing from the top of the deck, turn the cards face up one on top of another until an ace appears or there is a maximum of thirteen cards. Repeat the process until there are three piles of cards.

> Three Aces = Yes;
> Two Aces = Maybe;
> One Ace or None = No

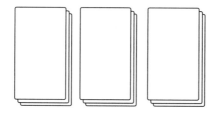

Layout 4:
The Nine Card Spread

This is a good general spread. Shuffle the cards and lay them out as shown in the diagram. The first horizontal row displays past events related to the question; the second displays present events; and the third, events that are likely to occur.

Past

| 1 | 2 | 3 |

Present

| 4 | 5 | 6 |

Future

| 7 | 8 | 9 |

Ages 11 and up
Layout 5: Celtic Cross Spread

Since the spread below—an Italian gypsy tradition—was passed down through my mother's family, the card placements differ slightly from the standard used today.

Card 1 represents the situation related to the question.

Card 2 represents that which crosses the situation for better or worse. This can be an obstacle of sorts, but often is something positive and necessary in order for things to progress.

Card 3 symbolizes the events that brought the situation into being.

Card 4 represents the immediate future. The time frame involved is usually a matter of days, but seldom over eight weeks.

Card 5 symbolizes past events that relate to the question.

Card 6 tells of the more distant future, and that which is likely to occur should the querent continue the present path.

Card 7 represents the querent's current environment

Card 8 shows how current relationships affect the situation, and how people view the querent.

Card 9 reflects the hopes and fears of the querent, and brings him to a conscious understanding of how negative or positive he really feels about the situation.

Card 10 represents the final outcome based on past and present events, underlying circumstances, and the actions of the querent.

Celtic Cross Spread

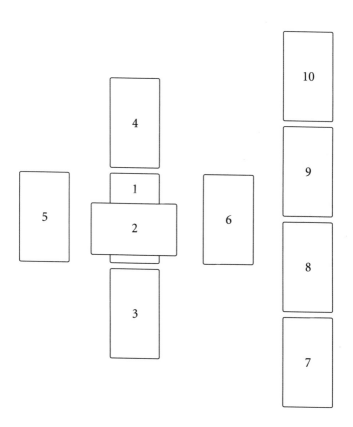

Ages 11 and up *(continued)*
Layout 6: The Wheel Spread

Card 1 represents the situation related to the question.

Card 2 represents that which crosses the situation for better or worse. This can be an obstacle of sorts, but often is something positive and necessary in order for things to progress.

Card 3 symbolizes the events that brought the situation into being.

Card 4 symbolizes past events that relate to the question.

Card 5 represents that which is likely to occur should the querent continue the present path.

Card 6 represents advice given to the querent in regard to the situation at hand.

Card 7 represents the querent's current environment.

Card 8 represents the final outcome based on past and present events, underlying circumstances, and the actions of the querent.

Wheel Spread

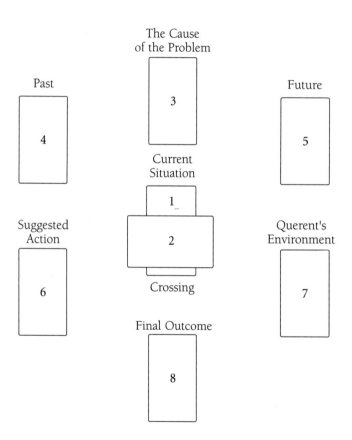

The Cause
of the Problem

3

Past

4

Future

5

Current
Situation

1

2

Suggested
Action

6

Querent's
Environment

7

Crossing

Final Outcome

8

Layout 7: Clarification Spread

Use the Clarification spread to gain more information from a reading. Since it is a modification of the Celtic Cross, the representations of Cards 1-10 as outlined in Layout 5 apply here, too. Cards 11-30 represent a more in-depth look at the information received from the first ten.

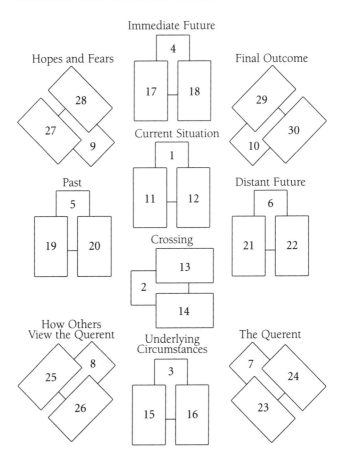

How To Use This Book

The following tips are offered to help you get the most from *The Whimsical Tarot*. While this may mean library outings or refreshing your memory on childhood literature, it's well worth the effort. You and your children will both enjoy the interaction. More important, though, you'll have the satisfaction of knowing that you've paved the path for your child's individual spiritual journey, and that's a gift as precious as life itself.

1. Give the card to your child, and let her tell you what he or she sees, feels, and hears.

2. Read the suggested story, poem, or nursery rhyme to your child. Some of the stories suggested are book length, however, and you may not wish to read the whole story to your child before working with the related card. In that case, tell your child about the characters depicted in the card as they relate to the suggested story.

3. Discuss the lessons of the story with your child. Answer any questions and listen to your child's comments.

4. Offer the card to your child again. Ask how the card makes him feel. Listen carefully to your child's comments, and write it all down. His or her responses will give you insight into the inner workings of your child and provide you with valuable parenting tools.

5. If necessary, go back to the section on Getting to Know the Deck, page 20, and help your child try the exercises.

6. Allow your child to pick a spread, lay out the cards (little ones may need help with this), and read them.

That's all there is to it! As your child is introduced to the magic of the Whimsical Tarot, take some time to rekindle the fairy-tale relationships you once cherished. One word of caution, though: Don't be surprised if you fall under the spell, too!

Part Two:

THE CARDS

We begin as The Fool on our personal paths
And travel our roads with joy, smiles, and laughs.
And then we progress to Magician from Fool
Learning new skills and working with tools.
We become the High Priestess and see the unseen;
Our mysteries are deep, our skills become keen.
As the Empress, we learn of abundance and love;
We create and we nurture both seedling and dove.
Rushing on as the Emperor, we grow and we change,
And we drink in his knowledge—the wisdom of age.
We progress as the Hierophant and learn of convention,
Of religion and status, and mindless tradition.
As the Lovers we learn of the matters of heart
Through the joys and the trials, we patiently sort.
Then we race as the Chariot, rushing quicker and faster.
We learn about balance and its principles, master.
Then hurled into Strength, we find not brute force,
But a subtler energy deep in its source.
When the Hermit takes over, we go deep inside
To the place where the spiritual self likes to hide.
Still traveling forward, we turn as the Wheel,
And learn to help others, as our luck we seal.
As Justice arrives, we progress as the scales;
We tip and we balance, then onward we sail
Into the Hanged One, where quickly we learn
Of spiritual balance, its importance; then turn
Into glorious Death and all that's involved
In beginnings, new growth, and old issues resolved.
As we become Temperance, we learn of control
And how much is too much. Still the energy flows
Until we're the Devil and break through our chains
And learn to go forward, accepting life's gains.

Then, as we break free, we change to the Tower,
And repair all relationships before they go sour.
Soon, we soar to the heavens. As the Star, we shine bright
And wishes come true in our joyful white light.

We fly to the Moon and we learn to watch out
For deceptions in life; then we go on about
Our business until we change into the Sun.
There we sip on life's nectar; we dance and we run
Until we find Judgment, and with it, we meld
And thoughts of unfairness are quickly dispelled
Then finally, at last, we rush toward the World
And the cycle is finished. Rewards are unfurled.
And though we are tired, we've accomplished our goal:
Achieving true balance of body and soul...

✿ ✿ ✿

The cards of the Major Arcana represent forces that affect our lives, but which are beyond our control. To a large degree, these forces shape the way life events play out. They represent a pattern or a series of steps that must be taken to get to a certain point. However, they do not necessarily affect its final outcome. That is solely up to us. We can either follow the outlined path, or change it to better suit ourselves.

The Major Arcana cards help us in a number of ways. They shed light on situations that we don't always understand. Things like a spell of bad luck, the appearance of someone unexpected, or a sudden reign of good fortune. They help us realize that we are not alone in this life—that unseen forces often help and hinder us—and that we are not necessarily at fault for everything that happens to us.

A spread comprised of many Major Arcana cards signifies the working of forces in our lives that we cannot see.

0 · The Fool

Character: The Scarecrow
Story: The Wizard of Oz

Description:

The Scarecrow is an excellent choice for depicting the Fool. The Fool is an open-minded sort, blessed with child-like innocence. He sees only beauty and adventure among the pitfalls of life, and he embraces them with joyful exuberance. He constantly seeks out the unknown, and explores endless possibilities. Everyone loves him. He's kind, courteous, caring, and fun to be around.

The problem with The Fool is that he simply doesn't think things through. Even if mundane thought were a possibility for him, it would mean having ideals, making a stand, or even more extreme, taking some kind of positive action to bring them into reality. Instead, he much prefers to float along in the clouds, allowing destiny to take him where it will. This, coupled with a naive and trusting nature, often gets The Fool into trouble.

Here we see the Scarecrow off on an adventure. The safety of his pole waits in the distance, and birds scavenge his untended crop. He veers from the yellow brick road to chase a butterfly. He hasn't a care in the world, and only sees the beauty just beyond his grasp. He doesn't realize there's a fire below the cliff's edge. Toto barks a warning. Will he listen or just keep chasing beauty?

Advice:

When The Fool skips through your spread, take time to smell the roses, and find the silver lining in the clouds overhead. Sing. Laugh. Be happy. Dance in the joy of being alive. Think back to your childhood, and recapture the innocence and purity of that time. Do some of the things you enjoyed as a child (play jacks, draw crayon pictures, make paper chains), and grab the inspiration that awaits you. Have some fun. Play a little. Delegate responsibility and find some free time. Open your mind and welcome new opportunity without worry.

Embrace your Spirit Guide, and let it take you where it will. What you find out about yourself on the spiritual level will delight and surprise you. It will also provide new insight into why you seem to make the same mistakes over and over.

List your dreams, then take action to bring them into reality. Ignore those who—though they have your best interest at heart—insist that your goals will never come to fruition. Have the pure, undoubting faith of a child, and reach out for your desires.

I · The Magician

Character: Puss 'N Boots
Story: Puss 'N Boots

Description:

A vine symbolizing "Akasha" or "Spirit" divides this card into upper and lower sections. Puss 'N Boots stands in the center of the card and cuts the sign of infinity in the air with his sword. The rod, sword, cup and pentacle pictured in the sections represent Air, Fire, Water, and Earth respectively. Puss 'N Boots is master of the elements. As he combines his knowledge with the elemental powers, he creates a strong magic that is of benefit to himself and to all around him.

Like Puss 'N Boots, The Magician is an enterprising person, one who uses what he knows to help himself and others. He has the ability to turn any bad situation around so that it becomes beneficial, rather than catastrophic. Sometimes the Magician is an occult figure, but he can also be a person with a quick mind, a strong constitution, and a love of challenge. Nothing passes the Magician unnoticed, and he sees nothing in this world as trivial. He knows that everything is important in the workings of the world, the spirit, and the cosmos. He is creativity personified.

Advice:

When you draw The Magician card, realize that you are a powerful person and that your natural talents are growing, living things. They are like a plant which must be tended, nurtured, and fertilized to bear fruit. Work with your talents to keep them strong and healthy. Harvest them, and learn to use their fruits to your best advantage. Accept challenges willingly. Find creative solutions to difficult situations. Think. Meditate. Use your intuition; its powers are great. Trust your inner voice, and act upon its advice. Find the reason for a problem even if none seems to exist. Thoroughly explore each predicament from every angle. Look at each piece of the puzzle. Pay attention to detail; even the smallest particle of information could have bearing on the situation. Find something good in every set of difficulties. Build upon the positive aspects for the best possible outcome. Keep a level head. Trust your judgment. Listen to the problems of others, and see what you can do to help them. Use your talents to find solutions that will benefit all concerned.

II · The High Priestess

Character: The Fairy Godmother
Story: Cinderella

Description:

Here we see Cinderella's Fairy Godmother slowly twirling about in the center of the Universe. Bubbles of colored light that represent the Element's flow from her wand as she gently divides the night from day, the dark from light, and the spiritual from the mundane. Even though her footsteps turn only on the weightlessness of ether, the expression on her face is peaceful, calm, and serene. This suggests that she has no cause for worry. After all, she is the High Priestess—a being who is totally in control of her balance and position between opposite worlds and dimensions.

Like the Fairy Godmother, the High Priestess is an omnipotent creature. All-knowing, all-seeing, and all-hearing, she holds each shred of magic, balance, and knowledge of the Universe in the palm of her hand. She knows when you're sad. She knows when you're happy. She is completely aware of your needs and wants. Best of all, the High Priestess is your friend. She knows what is best for you, and has workable solutions to all of your problems. While this wonderful creature is completely at your disposal and willing to help you, she offers nothing until you pay the price—swallowed pride and a sincere request for her assistance.

Advice:

The High Priestess is a very magical card and represents the balance between the spiritual and mundane worlds. When she makes an appearance, it usually means it's time to get your act together. Accept responsibility for your actions. Take control of your life and your surroundings. Stop depending upon others to make your decisions. Search for underlying causes for your present circumstances. Do you keep repeating the same mistakes over and over? Look for information that is hidden from view. Are you allowing outside forces to interfere with what is best for you? Listen to your intuition. Know that what your inner voice tells you is worth hearing and acting upon. Take a good look at the situation, and make a practical decision based on what you see.

This card can also suggest that you are either too firmly rooted in the mundane or floating too freely in the spiritual realm. If that is the case, take a good hard look at yourself and see where you're lacking. Find a comfortable balance point, then strike a happy medium.

III · The Empress

Character: The Old Woman in the Shoe
Nursery Rhyme: The Old Woman in the Shoe

Description:

In this depiction, we see the Old Woman in the Shoe feeding a baby. She is the picture of peace and serenity, even though many things are are going on around her. She doesn't worry that the kettle may boil over, or that the kids might get into the bread before supper time. She is totally unconcerned that someone is flying a kite from a bedroom window. She is focused only on the task at hand: sustaining and nurturing the tiny life that cuddles happily in her lap.

The Queen Mother of Nature, the Empress represents all that is nurturing, fertile, and abundant in our world. Note the flowers that sprout here and there, the roses and ivy vines that freely climb the walls of her home, and the lush green grass all about her. See how her children—a product of her own creative forces—entertain themselves quietly with life's simple pleasures. They have no need to tug on her sleeve or interrupt the baby's feeding time. They know that in due time, they'll each have a turn to reap the benefits of their mother's attention. Her love is rich and abundant, and there's plenty to go around.

Advice:

When The Empress graces you with her presence, feel the essence of femininity. Often a mother-figure or one who nurtures those in her circle of friends, The Empress can also represent a pregnancy or the birth of a new idea. She signifies all that is prosperous, abundant, and plentiful. Turn outward and embrace those around you. Give or listen to sound advice. Enjoy family atmosphere. Give those you love an extra dose of tender loving care. Give yourself an extra dose, too. Sow the seeds of inspiration, and plant new ideas. Nurture and fertilize the seedlings, and pluck out the weeds of doubt and disharmony. Tend your crop carefully, and bring it to full term. Harvest and act upon your ideas and their offshoots. Bring them into reality. Use them as a base for new projects. Expect your plans to come to fruition. Prosperity and abundance are yours, or will be soon. Share what you have with others. Take a few moments and meditate on Mother Earth and all she gives to you. Thank her for her bounty, her richness, and your life. Do something nice for her.

IV · The Emperor

Character: Santa Claus/Father Winter
Story: Discuss Santa Claus/Father Winter with your child.

Description:

Santa Claus/Father Winter knows all, hears all, and sees all. Nothing escapes him, not even the most trivial word or deed. For he is an all-encompassing, omnipotent force. He is everywhere at once. His snowy, long white hair and beard tell us he's old, but his ageless face belies the youthful outlook and flexibility necessary to get along in our ever-changing world. Though he bears the gifts of wisdom for all to see, the twinkle in his eye and pleased grin on his face tell us that he's keeping the really important stuff deep in the bottom of his bag. He's waiting to share it with you. All you have to do is ask.

The Emperor is a down-to-earth fellow with valuable advice to share. He's been there—done that. There's no situation that he hasn't encountered and successfully mastered. As proof, he wears the robe of spiritual richness and the cloak of physical growth. Understanding the need for the quiet, regenerative season of Winter, he walks slowly through the frozen lands. With each step, he gathers the collective wisdom of the Earth. It replenishes his energy and brings him new life.

Advice:

The Emperor comes to call when better-than-average "people" skills are necessary to resolve a situation. A powerful, stable, and secure person, he carries the wisdom of age. The Emperor is also somewhat of a father-figure, so when he turns up in a spread, ask the advice of someone who is older or wiser than you. Question those, too, who are younger but have the wisdom of experience. Speak little and listen much. Pay close attention to the advice, and listen as much to what is not said as to what is. Study the way your "advisor" lives his life. What is important to him? What is not? How does he handle the people around him? How does he care for them? What is it about his life that is different from yours? Study his actions, and learn from his attitude. Turn inward and take a good look at your spiritual self. Talk to your Spirit Guide. Open your mind, your heart, and your ears. Begin a spiritual house-cleaning. Search for the things that keep you from making good decisions, and get rid of them. Look at all the facts and how they connect to each other. Then make a decision based on that information.

V · The Hierophant

Character: Friar Tuck
Story: The Adventures of Robin Hood

Description:

Friar Tuck is not the sort of person that normally comes to mind when someone utters the phrase, "religious figure." He is a jolly fellow, enjoys a good skirmish now and then, and is not above pulling a good prank or two. A non-conformist, he much prefers freedom to the trappings of comfort that society deems necessary. He realizes the value of his own individuality, and scoffs at those who feel the need to be just like everyone else. His home is the forest, his family is a band of vagabonds known as Merry Men, and his friends are the many animals who populate the woodlands.

Here we see the good Friar in the midst of transformation. The forest changes around him. Autumn leaves pirouette from the trees. The grass remains green, signaling room for personal growth and fertility. The whole atmosphere is the picture of serenity, peace, and freedom.

Regardless of how free Friar Tuck might appear, though, he still wears the trappings of religious dogma, as symbolized by the monk's robe he dons. The Celtic Cross pendant, however, reminds the Friar that his freedom lies in the proper balance of the elements within himself. Facing eastward, he initiates personal change by raising his cup in salute to the sun—bringer of the new day and giver of warmth, health, and success. The sun shines upon him in return, illuminating his cup and face with its golden rays, and bringing him the motivation necessary to break his personal bonds of convention. Nearby, a squirrel nibbles an acorn (the fruit of the sturdy oak tree), suggesting that strength is often essential in achieving total liberation.

Advice:

The Hierophant is often seen as a religious figure, but more frequently represents a person who feels trapped by the traditions and rituals of everyday living. Just once, he'd like to do something irresponsible, unconventional, and not in keeping with his image. When the Hierophant comes to visit, free yourself of societal trappings, and do something just for fun. This doesn't mean, however, that you should break the laws of the land or put anyone in harm's way. Just be yourself, and do what's right for you. Realize that it doesn't matter what other people think or whether they approve of your actions. After all, they can't live your life. Go ahead, take a chance. Take back your life. It belongs to only you.

VI · The Lovers

Characters: Beauty and the Beast
Story: Beauty and the Beast

Description:

On a clear summer night, beneath the light of the full moon, a spell of love is in the making. The heady fragrance of spring flowers fills the air, and stars sparkle like diamonds in the sky. It's the perfect night for love and romance.

Beauty and the Beast waltz through the garden. They are of two distinctly different species—one fully human, and the other, a frightful sort of beast—but their hearts beat as one. The Beast, by nature, is strong, gruff, overbearing, and somewhat rough around the edges. Beauty is a delicate creature of gentle

48

sweetness, and emotion. Though complete opposites in temperament and appearance, they meet on the common ground of love. They each draw upon the personality traits of the other. Suddenly, the Beast no longer seems as frightening. His face takes on a softer quality and becomes almost handsome. He gives his strength and instinct to Beauty. She becomes more able to face and deal with future challenges in the world outside.

Because of the obvious differences between the Beast and Beauty, no one would expect this relationship to work. Their hardships will be many. Tears will flow. Together, though, they can overcome whatever obstacles block their path, for the power of love conquers all.

Advice:

Love is the most beautiful of the spiritual gifts, but often the most difficult to maintain. The Lovers whisper tenderly in your ear that romance, harmony, and true emotion are waiting just for you. When they dance into a spread, though, they also bring the tests of minor hardships and complications. These aggravations are a necessary part of any lasting relationship; for they build it, strengthen it, and give it spice. Reach out and take the heart offered to you. Love it, nurture it, and soothe it. Join with that heart, become a part of it, and let it become a part of you. Know that love balances all, and it's yours for the taking. But know, too, that love doesn't come without trials, tears, and misgivings. You must be willing to accept imperfection and human failing, and be up to the challenge. It's a little like a roller coaster ride. There are lots of unexpected twists and turns, and sometimes you feel like the bottom is going to drop out—but once you get back to solid ground, you realize that the end result made that funny feeling in the pit of your stomach well worth the effort!

VII · The Chariot

Character: The pumpkin coach
Story: Cinderella

Description:

Here we see Cinderella's pumpkin coach barreling down the cobblestone road toward home. The party is over now. The castle is dark. It's time to go back to the drudgery of real life, or so it seems. However, the light of full moon illuminates the path and falls over the verdant hills and valleys as a reminder that the mystery of magic always accompanies growth and change in our personal worlds.

Metamorphosis is magic, and such changes are now in progress. Note that the tree leaves on the left hand side of this card have changed to autumn colors, while those on the right hand side still reflect summer verdancy. The once-splendid coach and prancing horses have been replaced by a pumpkin drawn by a pair of mice. The mice, though harnessed together as a team, now hurriedly pursue individual paths. They race away from each other at breakneck speed. The fact that no driver appears in this depiction gives us pause for thought. What happened to him? Did he jump from the careening carriage and try to save himself? Or did he just wait for his own personal transformation, and allow the balance of Fate to choose his destiny?

Advice:

The Chariot is a card of growth, change, and transformation. It races in at the speed of light, then takes off again like a whirling dervish. When this card turns up in a spread, it represents the attraction of opposites to make a perfect whole. Even with distinctly different agendas, these opposites find themselves drawn to each other and forced into teamwork.

The Chariot also signifies business travel, more than likely involving ventures in areas not previously considered. Plans suddenly come together, take shape, and come to fruition, often in a most peculiar way. Prepare for side trips, roads less traveled, and the unexpected.

Above all, don't become overwhelmed with the amount of activity The Chariot brings. Take things as they come. If too many things happen at once, learn to prioritize. Handle the important items first, and catch up with the rest later. Do one thing at a time. Go with the flow. Keep your balance. Stay calm. Learn to be a team player. Ask for help if you need it. Then look for solutions to come from unexpected sources.

VIII · Strength

Character: Little Bo Peep
Nursery Rhyme: Little Bo Peep

Description:

At first glance, the scene depicted here seems to denote anything but strength. Here we see Little Bo Peep shield her eyes from the sun's glare as she searches the countryside for her sheep. The sheep slowly meander her way, but all is not well. A lone wolf perched on the hill above howls a warning to Bo Peep. He tells her to move on, to get out of his way, that supper is waiting, and he doesn't intend to lose it.

Though it's no easy feat, Bo Peep appears to be calm, cool, and collected. She stands her ground and shows no fear.

Further, she pretends not to notice the wolf or hear his warning. She knows this will disturb and distract the animal, for he is used to getting his way by using scare tactics to frighten others into retreat. It won't be long before the wolf will begin to question his personal ability to achieve goals and his authority in the world around him. And when that happens, he'll just give up, tuck his tail, and move on.

Little Bo Peep understands the psychology of strength. While brute force has its place, it seldom works as one would think. It's much more effective to plant a seed within the core of our adversaries—in this case, one of doubt—and nurture it into victory.

Advice:

When the Strength card appears in a spread, it doesn't mean to flex your muscles, puff out your chest, and take what you want by brute force. Rather than muscle power, this card denotes courage, bravery, and inner strength. If your present circumstances aren't happy ones, identify the problem. Go within and look for answers. Explore your options and look at your possibilities. See what you can do to rectify matters. Realize that people around you who aren't part of the solution are part of the problem. Disentangle them from your life. You are in control of your life, but only if you have the courage to take charge. Be brave enough to play the hand you've been dealt—and play it to your best ability, regardless of the consequences. Develop a subtle sort of strength—the kind that allows others to make their own mistakes and decisions without interference. Plant ideas to make your desires come to fruition; then sit back and wait quietly as they blossom.

IX · The Hermit

Character: The Sandman
Story: Tell your child about the Sandman
and his bag of sleep dust.

Description:

The Sandman is the eternal hermit. He only comes out to play when the rest of the world is safely in bed. Though we've never had the chance to hold him in pleasant conversation or even so much as caught a glimpse of him, we know he's our friend. Silently, he creeps through the night, going about his work. He brings us the gifts of peaceful guidance and creative dreaming.

The Sandman is an old soul, and he carries with him the wisdom of the ages. The unkempt appearance of his hair and beard denote retreat from civilization and the growth gained from inner search. To seal his invisibility, he wears a deep blue robe splashed with stars and moons, it is the perfect camouflage against the midnight sky.

Here we see the Sandman slipping through a casement window—a symbol of the gateway between the spiritual and physical—into the bedroom of a sleeping child. He reaches into his box of creative treasures, and sprinkles them in the direction of the child to ensure the inner peace of spirituality in a busy, hectic world.

Advice:

When the Hermit creeps into a spread, it's time to take a break from the mundane world and delve into the spiritual realm. Rest, relax, and take time for yourself. Recuperate from the business of life's everyday activities, and listen to your inner voice. Forget about society's expectations. Explore the options. Take your time. Don't rush into anything. If you're unsure of an offer, ask for clarification. Be certain you understand what the situation entails, then choose the path that is right for you.

Allow yourself to dream a little, and make plans for reaching your goals. Be creative. Only through dreaming can you live a fulfilling existence in the physical world.

Let your higher self take over, and pay close attention to what it has to say. Take its advice and begin the pilgrimage toward self-discovery. As you travel the path toward self, sort through your life and toss out any extraneous baggage. Realize that the inward search and spiritual house-cleaning is not always fun, but it is imperative to finding out who you really are, where your talents lie, and your purpose for existence in this life.

X · The Wheel of Fortune

Character: The flax plant
Story: The Flax

Description:

"The Flax" is the story of a tiny seed that grows, blossoms, and experiences many changes along the path of life. It learns to live as thread, cloth, napkins, and paper. It undergoes transformation by fire, and lives again as smoke. Finally, it becomes a vital and eternal part of the Earth's atmosphere. The little flax likens its life cycle to the song sung by the spinning wheel as it works.

Here, in the spokes of that wheel, we see the changes endured by the flax. We come to understand that in order to create, the old form must be destroyed. And just as the flax, we must undergo a constant transformative process to gain new life and achieve immortality. Unseen forces set the wheel of life into motion. Resistance is a waste of energy, and only makes life difficult for us. We must sing to the rhythm of life and learn to dance its steps, for the song never stops.

The wheel of life turns round and round. Good fortune comes our way, then just as we get comfortable, a run of bad luck clouds our existence. For this reason, going with life's flow isn't always easy. The changes of The Wheel are constant. They aren't always pleasant at the onset, but they benefit us in the end.

Advice:

When the Wheel of Fortune turns up in a spread, prepare for beneficial change. Not every experience will bring immediate pleasantness, but the lessons involved are filled with generous rewards. So be joyful as each new adventure unfolds, no matter how it looks at the onset. Each shift of the wheel brings new concepts, new life, and new meaning to your existence. Let go of your old life. Accept each change— no matter how challenging—with a smile. Allow yourself to be transformed into what you were born to be.

Be nice to those who are down on their luck. Give your old clothes to the homeless shelter. Volunteer at the local hospital. Give away hugs and smiles (we all have plenty of those). Make a point of saying something nice to someone. Be supportive. You never know how something you say or do might affect someone else. Your words or deeds could give someone the courage to take charge of their life and change their situation. Remember, someday you might walk in their shoes and need someone to help you.

XI · Justice

Characters: Goldilocks and Baby Bear
Story: Goldilocks and the Three Bears

Description:

Entering a home without the owner's permission shows little respect for fellow human beings or their property. Eating someone else's food without asking is extremely rude. But sleeping, uninvited, in someone else's bed really compounds matters. In fact, if one of us did those things today, we'd be charged with trespassing, breaking and entering, theft, and other crimes too numerous to mention. It might be said that because the victims were bears, none of this applies. It does. Goldilocks knew better. By her actions, she exhibited a complete disregard for others and their belongings. Thus, she must pay the consequences.

In this picture, Goldilocks sits up in a bed adorned in green, symbolizing the personal growth gained from justice. Baby Bear points her out to the constable. Goldilocks' eyes widen in horror. It's not because she's afraid of the bear. She simply can't believe she's been caught. She's always taken what she wanted. This time, though, she can't charm her way to freedom. There's no place to run. At long last, Goldilocks is forced to accept responsibility for her actions, and pay for her crimes against the Earth's creatures.

Advice:

The Justice card usually graces a spread when fair play is an issue. This might involve the legal system, a court battle, or righting some wrong that's occurred. In certain cases, it could also represent a karmic debt that's currently due and payable. Remember that the scales of justice are impartial, and there is no favoritism. Unfairness never escapes their clutches. Rich or poor, young or old—no one is passed over. There are no gray areas or extenuating circumstances, only balance.

The laws of justice are simple. Be considerate. If it isn't yours, don't take it. Accept responsibility for your own actions. If you make a mistake, admit it and say you're sorry. Help others when you can, but know the difference between interference and assistance. Practice the golden rule.

Stand up for yourself and for what you believe, no matter the consequences. Have the courage of your convictions. Strive to treat everyone fairly, yourself included, and the scales will always tip in your favor.

XII · The Hanged One

Character: The Fishwife
Story: The Little Gold Fish
(also known as "I Beg a Wish of the Magic Fish")

The Hanged One

XII

Description:

Here we see the fishwife hanging upside down with one foot caught fast in a fish net. This is her punishment for insatiable greed. While she still lives in the physical world, her body hangs in suspended animation to mark the balance between the spiritual and the mundane. Her feet point toward the sky and her head hangs near the ocean. The Universe whispers softly in assurance, for she now has exactly what she desired. She is, indeed, the Queen of the Sun and the Moon and the Stars.

Dressed in the spiritual colors of purple and white, the fishwife also wears a red shawl to represent the mundane. Her determined face is now expressionless, the greed and lust once there are replaced by inner peace. She is quite content as she swings in the sea air, for her place in the Universe is now defined. She no longer has problems. She no longer has worries. Interruptions are at a standstill. All she hears are the spiritual mysteries that echo from the shell in her hand, and the lullabye of the ocean as its tides rise and fall below her.

Advice:

The Hanged One is a very spiritual card. It reminds us that we need to look at both sides of life (the spiritual and the physical) with equal interest, and balance them accordingly. If you've been too caught up in life's rat race to pay much attention to your higher self, take a break. Close the windows, lock the doors, and unplug the telephone. Block out all mundane disturbances. Relax. Allow yourself some quiet time. Step back and look at things with a fresh eye, a different perspective. Take time to smell the roses.

Meditate upon the reasons for your birth, your present life, and your role in the universal plan. Realize that you hold an integral strand in the cosmic web, and that without you, the world, as we know it, would cease to exist. Understand that you make a difference. Care for the spiritual body as you do the physical one. Soothe it. Love it. Nurture it. Bring it back into balance. Only then will you see things as they really are.

XIII · Death

Character: Sleeping Beauty
Story: Sleeping Beauty

Description:

In this card, we see Sleeping Beauty lying in peaceful repose on her bed as a mouse chatters nearby to wake her up. The cobwebs in the picture tell us she's been there for a very long time. In fact, to the physical eye she appears dead, but we know that isn't so. She is simply lying in state; waiting for the rest of her life to take shape, unfold, and blossom.

Her long wait is nearly over. Sunshine, with its promise of new life, pours golden radiance through the nearby window. The green of her gown denotes growth, and the yellow of her sleeves and sash suggest that creativity and fresh perspective are afoot. The roses she holds are fresh, luscious, and vibrant as their heady perfume meanders through her peaceful slumber, and stirs new life into the crevices of her subconscious. It travels deep inside, telling her that someday soon she will run, play, and dance again, that she'll be able to do all the things she's missed so much. However, Sleeping Beauty's new life will hold much more. Adventure, experience, and discovery await. So does the opportunity to make a difference. All she has to do is open her eyes, sieze the moment, and make a firm resolution to avoid her past mistakes.

Advice:

Contrary to popular belief, the Death card is nothing to fear. Rejoice when it turns up in a spread, for it heralds the beginning of a new era. Prepare for the close of a chapter in your life, and joyfully accept the opportunity to go on to something different. This might involve the end of an unhealthy relationship, a period of depression, or the conclusion of a set of unsettling events.

When you draw this card, it's time for a mental housecleaning. Sweep away the cobwebs, and throw out all the garbage cluttering your mind. Discard old, outdated ideas to make room for new ones. Get rid of musty anger, moldy grudges, and the filth of old heartache. Raise the windows, open the doors, and look for light at the end of the tunnel. Expect something fresh, new and exciting, then turn the page. Be reborn, and rejoice in your new life.

XIV · Temperance

Characters: Jack and Jill
Nursery Rhyme: Jack and Jill

Description:

Here we see Jack and Jill rolling down a grassy knoll. The roots of their plight are many (a lack of attention, a lack of patience, the need to hurry through their chores in an effort to get back to their childhood play). They all add up to a lack of balance, which is ultimately the key factor in their chaotic tumble.

The well house symbolizes the source of the waters of life; the ever-flowing, ever-changing liquid that maintains the balance between the physical and spiritual worlds. The beehive represents the Universal Plan and the natural order of moderation that we must follow in order to exist in both worlds successfully. Had Jack and Jill adhered to this natural order, they wouldn't be in such a mess. As a result, they will have to dust themselves off, return to the well house, and repeat their task until they're able to complete it properly.

Will Jack and Jill be able to get past the bees and successfully return with the bucket of water? The frog reminds them of their tendency to hurry through life, but the cool blue of their well-worn overalls assures them that they possess the calmness necessary to achieve their goal. All they have to do is collect their wits, stay on an even keel, and remember that patience and moderation are the best policies.

Advice:

The Temperance card warns that too much of a good thing is hazardous. When this card graces a spread, remember that moderation is the key to healthy living. Slow down. Take your time. It doesn't matter whether you reach your destination in five minutes, five hours, five days, or even longer. Have a little patience with yourself and those around you. Remember that we all make mistakes from time to time. We also have a tendency to make more out of our errors than is necessary, and to expect more from ourselves than is humanly possible.

Keeping that in mind, balance discipline with love, and criticism with kindness. When things look darkest, look for that single ray of hope hiding in the clouds. Balance your physical life, too. If you need quick solutions to tricky problems, try meditation. Evaluate the circumstances, and think before you act.

XV · The Devil

Characters: The Puppet Master and Pinnochio
Story: Pinnochio

Description:

Here we see Pinnochio performing onstage. Of course, his every move is solely the whim of the wicked Puppet Master. A pull of the strings, and Pinnochio dances. Another tug, and he bows. The puppeteer is having the time of his life. He loves the rush. He loves the power. He loves the feeling that comes from controlling everything and everyone around him. It makes him feel as if he rules the world, and in a sense, he does.

While it may seem appropriate to feel sorry for Pinnochio, he doesn't deserve our pity. To begin with, he wouldn't be in this mess at all if he had stayed at home with people who loved and cared for him. His problems are merely the manifestation of his own faulty decision-making. However, they don't have to last forever. Pinnochio is still the master of his own fate. He has the ability to change his personal reality, and can break free of the Puppet Master any time he wishes to do so. All he has to do is use his head, summon some gumption, and stop feeding the Puppet Master's greed. Reclaiming his life and going back home is just a snip or two away. It's only a matter of snatching the scissors from his back pocket and slicing through the strings.

Advice:

The Devil represents the limits we set for ourselves, the chains with which we bind ourselves, and the mental weapons we use against ourselves to keep from getting ahead. We hold ourselves hostage by refusing to let go of fear, desire, and lack of initiative. When this card comes up in a spread, free yourself by taking a step toward betterment. Let go of fear. Trash any old ideas that are not to your benefit. Rid yourself of greed. Separate yourself from debilitating relationships. Lose everything negative in your life. Doing so tears down the fences holding you back, and supplies you with a limitless source of opportunity and possibility. Accept inspiration, and embrace new concepts. Believe in yourself and your abilities. Know that you can do whatever it takes to be the person you want to be. Take some initiative. Act upon your dreams. Flap your wings a few times and spread them. Then, fly a little. You'll never know how far you can go unless you try.

XVI · The Tower

Characters: The Three Little Pigs and the Big Bad Wolf
Story: The Three Little Pigs

Description:

The three little pigs each had separate construction ideas when it came to building houses. Only one of them had sense enough to build a fortress that guaranteed safe living. Try as he might, he could not convince the other two to follow suit. Now, he and his brother watch helplessly as the big bad wolf completely destroys the straw home of their sibling with a single puff of air. Sadly, their brother's life is now on the line because he wouldn't listen.

The wolf in this card represents the Cosmos, while his breath signifies the unseen forces that accompany its realm. The three little pigs symbolize all of humankind. Together, they remind us that we must take the reins on life's path, and tend to our own measures of security. We, like the endangered pig, know that nothing can stand the test of time without a solid foundation. That doesn't deter us from moving on with things, though. Just as the pig, we become stubborn, impatient, and hurry through important issues without giving one thought to the consequences. What shall become of us if we continue in this manner? Will we end up like the pig? Or will we be able to bail ourselves out before it's too late?

Advice:

When The Tower turns up in a spread, expect a commotion. This card represents shock, collapse, and destruction. Sometimes it signifies an abrupt and unexpected move of residence, and the loss of personal possessions and property. More frequently, though, it applies to relationships, communications, and emotions. This card is a reminder that nothing lasts forever unless it is built on a solid foundation. Check for "cracks" in the foundations of relationships, partnerships, and personal associations. Mend them before complete reconstruction becomes necessary. If an apology is in order, make it. If hurt feelings are an issue, soothe them. Straighten out any misunderstandings before emotional turmoil gets out of control. If you suspect that someone might mistake your words or actions to mean something other than your original intention, take the time to clarify your feelings on the matter. Make a mental note to say what you mean and mean what you say. Be honest and forthright in your relationships, and avoid any misunderstanding that might cause a rift later.

XVII · The Star

Character: The Blue Fairy
Nursery Rhyme: Star Light, Star Bright

Description:

Here we see a small girl sitting on the bank at dusk. Like other children the world over, she awaits the first star of evening. In their eyes, it's the most valuable star in the sky. Practically speaking, it heralds the coming of night—a time of rest and relaxation, peace and quiet. But more important to the children is the magic that it holds. The first star of the evening, the wishing star, is the star that makes all goals possible and makes dreams come true.

As the child waits with anticipation, the Blue Fairy begins her magical performance. She closes her eyes, concentrates, and quickly rubs her hands together. The warmth between her palms grows. The heat intensifies. Suddenly, a tiny spark appears. The fairy opens her eyes and moves her hands apart. As she does, the energy moves upward, downward, and out. The spark burns larger, stronger, and brighter. Soon it will light up the sky with its fiery twinkle, and alert children everywhere that she is present. They will know the time has come—the magical time they all await. The time has come to wish upon that tiny star, and have their dreams come true.

Advice:

The Star links the past and future, bringing them together with freshness of form and perspective. When this card appears, it's time to take a look at who we are, who we want to be, where we're going, and how the blending of the spiritual and physical can help us reach our goals. Take account of your personal balance between the physical and the spiritual. For it's only through equalization of the two that you become who you are meant to be. Look at your past, and collect successful strategies to help you gain your desires. Work to fulfill hopes, dreams, and wishes. View them with a fresh eye, and from a different angle. Turn them over and over in your mind until you find the spiritual keys to their fulfillment. Trust your intuition. Call upon your inner muse for inspiration. Seize the creativity given, and use it wisely. Imagine your dreams coming true, and visualize any related events exactly as you wish them to happen. Open yourself up to receive all that life has to offer you.

XVIII · The Moon

Characters: The cow, dog, dish and spoon
Nursery Rhyme: Hey Diddle Diddle,
the Cat and the Fiddle

Description:

It all started out as a moonlit picnic. The dog thought it was a splendid idea, so he gathered his favorite food, some eating utensils, and a festive table cloth. He had found a great spot, quiet and peaceful—the perfect place to kick back and enjoy his meal. But then something happened. The cow who'd been grazing peacefully across the way suddenly got a funny look in her eye. Then she gathered momentum, and jumped right over the Moon!

Here we see the dog entranced by the magic of the spectacle. Absolutely mystified, he can't believe his eyes. He wonders how the cow managed to fly, for she has no wings. He wonders what it's like up there amongst the moon and stars. Then he wonders if he could do it, too. Maybe if he mustered up enough strength, speed, and courage, he could join her in the fun.

While he's lost in the magic of the moment, we look on helplessly. We watch as everything he holds dear in life changes, transforms, and gains new life. Food, dishes, and eating utensils sprout legs. They run away. In one quick moment, life as he knows it has come to an end, simply because he failed to pay attention.

Advice:

The appearance of The Moon usually signifies that you haven't been paying attention to what's going on around you. While distraction holds its pleasantries, now is not the time to daydream. The mists of deception are settling in all around you. Shake off that wide-eyed wonder, and stop baying at the moon. Square your shoulders, get moving, and take care of business. Examine your situation. Are people taking advantage of you? Taking credit for your work? Stepping over you on their way up the ladder of success? Maybe even stealing your personal possessions? Look closely at your situation, and make careful decisions.

It's also possible that unseen forces are wreaking havoc in your life. Are you always tired and worn out even though your health is fine? Do you feel like something is constantly zapping your energy supply? There could be a problem with the connection between your physical and spiritual selves. If you suspect this is the case, turn inward and investigate; then balance your worlds equally.

XIX · The Sun

Character: Tinkerbell
Story: Peter Pan

Description:

Though Tinkerbell plays a very important role in the story of Peter Pan, we seldom get a really good look at her. A constant source of movement, she flits to and fro so quickly that she's often depicted only as a tiny, flickering ball of white light. This is because the Sun is her mentor and the source of her power and exuberance.

Here we see Tinkerbell in her natural environment—a bed of daisies (the flowers of eternal youthfulness and innocence). She stops for a moment to honor the Sun and present Him to all who pass by. Illuminating her tiny frame with His radiant light, the Sun imbues her with His gifts. She holds her arms high in embrace, and the smiling Sun shines down upon her.

Tinkerbell stands there for a moment. Basking in the golden warmth, she feels vital and vibrant again. She smiles as a sudden burst of energy surges through her body, for this means that her magical powers have been renewed and replenished. She knows that she only has to believe, and all her dreams will come true. As the Sun looks on with a wink, we know that our dreams will, as well.

Advice:

The Sun is a very lucky card to turn up in a spread. When this card appears, it signifies that everything's going your way. Celebrate your triumphs and accomplishments, no matter how small. Bask in the sun, dance in the rain. Know that you now have the power to fulfill all your dreams. Revel in the workings of the Universal Plan, and delight in the way it's turned your life around. Thank the unseen forces in your life. Rejoice in the sheer pleasure of being alive. Be happy and relish life's little treasures. Do more than just smell the flowers, instead take time to deeply inhale the sweet perfume of life.

Be aware of all the good things in your life (good friends, good health, good luck), and draw upon that goodness to inspire future success. The vibrations of The Sun are contagious, so share your joy. Warm others with your exuberance. Your warmth and happiness could be their incentive for personal success.

XX · Judgment

Character: The Cricket
Story: Pinnochio

Judgment

XX

Description:

Though the story of Pinnochio is an enchanting tale, the main character would amount to very little without his friend, the Cricket. In fact, some believe that it is the Cricket's magic alone that makes the puppet a real boy. That's because he took it upon himself to teach the child about the human factors of responsibility, emotion, and love. His most difficult feat, however, was in helping Pinnochio gauge the difference between right and wrong, something we all must learn in order to interact successfully in the real world.

Here we see the Cricket perched in his normal position on Pinnochio's shoulder. Acting as his conscience, he whispers in his ear. "This is not right," he says. "You know what you must do." As Pinnochio shrugs him off, the Cricket becomes stubborn, tenacious, and persistent. He steps closer to the ear, cups his hands around his mouth, and raises his voice. He insists that he be heard—that his message gets through—and he doesn't care what price he has to pay. He understands that personal cost is of no consequence. For he is the conscience, the voice of reason, and the basis for sound judgment.

Advice:

Sound judgment comes from the little voice in our heads that whispers solutions when we are in doubt. When Judgment appears in a spread, it's usually an indication that we need to listen to our inner voice and act upon its advice. Often, the solutions offered by the conscience aren't easily carried out, and involve actions that seem awkward, humbling, and embarrassing. For that reason, we tend to ignore it and brush it aside. After all, it's human nature to look for the easy way out. Unfortunately, this attitude only complicates matters and makes life more difficult.

Pay attention to your conscience. Don't simply do as you please. No matter how disturbing the advice, do what you know is right. Greater consequences await you if the karmic team of cause and effect must be called upon. Their laws can be painfully ugly, heart-wrenching, and might even land you in court. Act fairly. Use sound judgment. Your conscience will sleep peacefully and never bother you again.

XXI · The World

Character: Glinda, the Good Witch of the South
Story: The Wizard of Oz

Description:

Glinda, the Good Witch of the South, has the magical ability to bring us everything we desire in this life. After all, she has experience. Through her efforts, the Scarecrow got a brain and the Tin Man, a heart. The Cowardly Lion got a dose of courage and Dorothy gained the power to get back home. She managed to give them every tool they lacked to move forward in life and successfully reach their goals. All they had to do was put those tools to use.

In this depiction, we see the mundane desires of Dorothy, the Lion, the Scarecrow, and the Tin Man represented by red slippers, a laurel wreath, a book, and a heart. We also see Glinda floating along in her bubble, a three-dimensional circle and symbol of the spiritual world. Even though the bubble tips and twirls as it travels, the good witch remains calm, collected, and balanced—a sure sign that all is well in her realm. Wand in hand, she looks at us expectantly, and patiently awaits our messages, questions, and requests. She cannot help us unless we ask. But once we do, Glinda is happy to pull out all the stops and give us the world. She can help us attain our strongest desires.

Advice:

No better card can float through a spread than The World. It indicates the achievement of perfect balance between the physical and spiritual realms, and that's what we're all trying to accomplish. It means you have the world by the tail, so to speak, and that all your goals are now within reach. Everything is in place. All you have to do is tie up the loose ends. Look at all the facets of the situation, and find a way to blend them together. It may take a little work, but you can handle it. If you need help, call upon forces seen and unseen, keeping the balance between the spiritual and physical. Look at each piece of the puzzle, then meditate upon finding its perfect fit. When the answers come, carefully put each piece properly in place. This is not as difficult as it sounds. You have the tools. You are the Master. The real difficulties and complexities are past you now. Take action. Complete the cycle. Wait for your dreams to come to fruition.

The Minor Arcana

Unlike the Major Arcana, we must take responsibility for the appearance of every Minor Arcana card that turns up in a spread. These cards signify matters over which we have total control. They represent our reactions to certain events, circumstances we develop for ourselves, and the way we handle our problems. The Minor Arcana cards also offer us choices; often without showing us the outcome. They point out past mistakes and possible scenarios of the future. Whether we learn from our mistakes or allow personal history to repeat itself is our decision.

The Minor Arcana cards are important because they give us a clear picture of who we are and where we stand. They temporarily remove us from situations to which we're too close, and allow us to take a step back to see them more objectively. Viewing ourselves from this angle, we see our faults, our qualities, and our talents. We see what we lack for success, and where we overcompensate. What's more, we see the reasons why. Through this painless form of objectivity, we enable ourselves to make solid, rational decisions about our personal paths and the future.

Many Minor Arcana cards in a spread signify that we are in control of our lives and our decisions, and that we must take responsibility for our own actions.

The Suit of Swords

Because of the heat necessary to forge metal, Swords represent the importance of Fire in our world. Fire heats, expands, energizes, purifies, seals, and is the major source of human passion. In the physical world, it is represented by sunshine, starlight, flame, electricity, nuclear power, and laser light.

Fire is ruled by the Sun, the source of warmth beneficial to all human existence. The power of Fire is tremendous, and not easily restrained. When out of control, the same properties that benefit us can harm, burn, or even kill. Because of this dynamic energy, Swords signify aggressive action. They protect us and advise of impending danger or aggravation. They alert us to be ready to defend what is ours. A spread comprised of many Swords signifies warning. Remember that Swords, like Fire, must be handled with caution, for they have the propensity to bring both victory and harm.

The borders of climbing thorny red roses of the cards of this suit indicate both the beauty and danger we encounter on our personal paths. They remind us that we live in an imperfect world, and that true human accomplishment comes only through careful planning, compromise, and sacrifice.

King of Swords

Character: The Woodcutter
Story: Little Red Ridinghood

Description:

Ruling as the King of Swords, the Woodcutter claims dominion over the power of the mind and all it entails. Since he rules both sides of the brain, he is equally responsible for both conscious and unconscious thought patterns. This means he feels just as at home in the intellectual world as he does in the psychic realm.

Because of his connection with Fire, this King is a quick-witted and powerful opponent. He frequently uses his intellect to outsmart his adversaries, then makes his point with aggression and speed. For this reason, he is often found in professional circles, and may choose the medical, legal, or corporate fields as his main source of support.

The King of Swords certainly doesn't mind luxury, but it isn't central to his survival. A basic life—one without bells, whistles, or the trappings of excess baggage—is much more to his liking. Living in such a way not only clears and sharpens his mind, but hones his ability to trod the cutting edge with great success.

Advice:

When the King of Swords marches through a spread, it's time to stop following your heart and use your head. Rely on your real power, your intellect, and let it guide you through the tricky situations at hand. Stand your ground, and use common sense to make your point. Know that aggressive action and radical change may be necessary to rectify the problems in question. Don't hesitate. Create a game plan, and follow through. Temper any aggression with politeness, though. You may need help, and others are much more likely to come to your aid when presented with a pleasant attitude instead of a surly one.

The appearance of this King may also denote a career change, especially if your present occupation leaves you with too much time on your hands. Look into a more challenging field. Think about what you'd really like to do, then explore your options. Don't worry that you might not have the proper qualifications. If additional education is necessary, consider going back to school. Once back in an academic setting, flex your brain muscles. Pay attention and put your mind into learning mode. Seek the life you want, and claim it for your own.

Queen of Swords

Character: Little Red Ridinghood
Story: Little Red Ridinghood

Queen of Swords

Description:

Little Red Ridinghood rules as the Queen of Swords, and has dominion over wisdom, personal defense and strategy, determination, and tenacity. Though she co-rules the psyche with the King of Swords, it is her voice that warns you of impending danger just before things go awry. She is also responsible for the little red flags that crop up in your brain from time to time; the ones that signal you to stop, look, and listen before you take any sort of action.

While this Queen also has an aggressive nature, she fully understands the strength of feminine charm. For this reason, she never just takes what she wants. Instead, she graciously allows others to think it was their idea to present her with it. She has a knack for managing people, thus she is often found at the top of executive and corporate ladders.

The Queen of Swords is somewhat of a loner. She prefers to keep others at a distance, and seldom lets them into her heart. Once her trust is gained, though, she responds with a firm commitment of loyalty and friendship.

Advice:

When the Queen of Swords steps into a spread, it usually means that your life is controlling you, instead of the other way around. Take stock of where you are in life, how you got there, and what you hope to gain from your present path. Think about your hopes, goals, and aspirations. Can you achieve them effectively from where you sit? Or do they always seem to be just out of arm's reach? If it's a case of the latter, take charge of your life. Turn your focus to what you want and need, then take the necessary steps to achieve it. You have the power to change your personal reality, but nothing positive can manifest until you stop dreaming and take action.

Rely on your natural gifts. Start with your intellect. It's a force to be reckoned with, and it holds the key to all you desire. Got a stubborn streak? Give it some exercise, too. Turn it into unshakable determination, and channel its energy toward your goals. Then, for once, do something your way. The outcome will surpass your wildest imagination.

Sometimes, this card brings an urge to control everyone else's life, too. Should this be the case, restraint is in order. Concentrate on your life, and let others handle their own. Instead of interfering, allow your good example to be the catalyst that gets others back on track.

Knight of Swords

Characters: Brer Fox and the Tar Baby
Story: Brer Rabbit and the Tar Baby

[Tales from Uncle Remus]

Knight of Swords

Description:

No doubt about it. Brer Fox is a smart guy. In fact, he's probably the most intelligent character in Uncle Remus' briar patch. But no matter how he schemed, he could never seem to get the upper hand on Brer Rabbit. At least, not until today.

Here we see the crafty Fox deeply engrossed in creativity. After dreaming up ways to pull a fast one on Brer Rabbit, he's finally come up with an idea. Not just a mediocre one this time, but a real dandy. Of course, the idea in question is to create the Tar Baby!

Now, Brer Fox isn't fond of looking foolish. In fact, it's his least favorite thing in world. So he puts his plans to paper first, to see if they'll work. He adjusts, revises, and irons out all the bugs. He works long into the day to make sure that they're absolutely perfect—positively foolproof—because the last thing he wants is to get caught at this mischief and wind up with egg on his face.

Advice:

When the Knight of Swords leaps into your spread, it's time to get off your duff and get busy. Timely matters are calling your name. In fact, if you don't hurry up and get with the program, you just may lose out.

Now is the time for aggressive action. Not sure what to do or which way to turn? Take a moment and clear your head. Rely on your creative force and the power of your intellect. Allow the ideas to flow freely, and write them down as they filter through. Then check your list carefully. Even if nothing on the list provides a workable solution, something there will at least prompt a clue as to the proper strategy.

Chart your course of action carefully. Check it over for flaws, and allow for possible error. If necessary, lay things out on paper. Treat this as a jigsaw puzzle, and make sure that each piece fits seamlessly into the next. If not, work with them until they do.

Then give some thought to your motives for the plan of action you've chosen. Are they simply self-serving? Or do they satisfy the needs of all involved? Once you're sure your vision meshes with the big picture, don't delay any longer. Set your plans into motion. You'll be glad you did!

Page of Swords

Depiction: An old-fashioned telescope

Page of Swords

©2000USGAMES

Description:

In days of old, the telescope was a very important tool. It was valuable to sailors, warriors, castle guards, and just about anyone else you could think of. It brought the range of vision close enough to find land on the open sea. It brought trespassers into sight. It even helped locate enemy troops as they hid amid brush and brambles. Its main use was in putting an end to the unknown presence, and for that reason, it helped promote measures of safety and security.

As wonderful as all that was, however, use of the telescope wasn't just confined to military and sea-faring personnel. Anybody could obtain one, and soon, people began using them for other reasons. They watched their neighbors at play, at work, and in the privacy of their homes. It wasn't long before the telescope achieved household status, and became commonly known as the "spy glass."

Here we see a beautiful rendering of an antique telescope. The blossoming roses are a reminder that this tool can be used to make life much sweeter. The ivy vines that twirl about its frame bring a famous Shakespearean line to mind: "Oh what a tangled web we weave, when first we practice to deceive."

Advice:

When the Page of Swords slips into a spread, it's time to take note of what's going on around you. Chances are, there's a spy in your midst, and someone's watching your every move. Take care to guard your privacy, your innermost secrets, and anything else you might not wish to share with the world. Hush. Be still. This is not the time for idle chatter. The things you say now may be misconstrued later. Instead, listen much. In doing so, you may gain valuable information that will help you later. Open your eyes. Watch your step. Look for clues as to how others perceive you. You never know what you may discover.

Although it may be difficult, don't let paranoia sneak in. It's a nasty monster, and over time, it can ruin your life. In this case, the strongest protection against its invasion is to be the best possible person you can be. Strive to live each day without doing the slightest bit of harm to anyone else. Be kind and generous. Behave appropriately. Set good examples and be the sort of person that everyone wants to emulate. Living in this fashion not only steals the spy's thunder, but crushes paranoia before it takes hold. Best of all, it makes you a better person.

Ten of Swords

Character: Humpty Dumpty
Nursery Rhyme: Humpty Dumpty

Ten of Swords

Description:

Humpty Dumpty isn't very smart. It's not his fault, though. The fact is, he doesn't have much of a brain. He's only an egg—an undeveloped embryo—and hasn't had the life experience that breeds intelligence and practical thinking. So when he climbed up on the castle wall, he didn't worry that anything bad might happen. He had no clue that his round exterior could not rest safely on a flat surface. And it certainly never occurred to him that he might slip and fall, causing his own demise. The only thing on his mind at the time was the beautiful sunset. He simply wanted to sit high enough to get a bird's eye view.

Here we see Humpty Dumpty falling in mid-air. A pile of jagged stones lies in wait below. The wall peg has already claimed a piece of his shell. It's an awful situation, but what can he do? There's nothing safe to hold on to, and nothing to brace his fall. All he can do is accept his fate, and hope there's some measure of relief at the end.

Advice:

If the Ten of Swords steals into your spread, prepare yourself for the worst. Disaster is at hand, and there's nothing you can do about it. Your best bet at this point is to just sit back and let it run its course.

If the failure is not of your own making, chill out. Do not beat yourself up over it. Just pick up the pieces and go on. If that's not the case, carefully explore the chain of events that led up to this awful mess. Then, take a good, hard look at your role in the affair. Do this with an objective eye, and the faulty links will show themselves with perfect clarity. You'll understand where things went wrong and why. You'll also come away with a clearer understanding of how such a problem might be prevented in the future. The key here is to learn from your mistakes so you won't inadvertently repeat them. In doing so, you may also prevent future heartache for yourself.

This card may also represent personal loss and betrayal at the hands of a trusted friend. Understand that those who stab you in the back for personal gain are not worth your energy or effort. Don't even bother to confront them. The best thing you can do is to give them a wide berth and stay far, far away from them.

Nine of Swords

Character: Rapunzel
Story: Rapunzel

Nine of Swords

Description:

Poor Rapunzel! Confined to the tower for what seemed like eternity, she spent most of her life without love, laughter, or companionship. In fact, the high point of the day came when her wicked captor screamed, "Rapunzel! Rapunzel! Let down your hair!" and climbed her massive tresses for a visit. As a result, Rapunzel became depressed, despondent, and very, very, sad.

If Rapunzel hadn't been so wrapped up in her own misery, she might have realized that she wasn't trapped. She might have seen that she had options—ways to change her personal reality and emerge as the victor. Unfortunately, she much preferred clinging to hopelessness and a "woe-is-me" attitude.

Here we see Rapunzel in tears. A pair of scissors rests on the table, and her golden locks hang heavily on the wall peg. Doesn't she see that she can climb down now? For that matter, didn't she realize that escape was within her grasp all along? She only had to cut her own hair—or chew it off, if necessary—to free herself and claim the life she wished for.

Advice:

When the Nine of Swords appears in your spread, it's time to stop whining about your problems and do something about them. Take back your life and gain some control. Don't like your personal reality? No problem. Reach down inside and grab all that makes you an individual. Combine those traits with a few creative thoughts and a hefty dose of determination. They're all you need to change your life.

Be yourself. Don't get caught up in the mutterings of society. Dare to be different. Don't stifle your individuality and creativity to pacify others. Exercise them instead. Learn to love yourself as you are and take your place as a unique strand of the Cosmic web. It's much easier and more fun than trying to fit the mold of society's expectations.

Know that inner struggles, no matter how difficult they may seem, are usually the product of a lack of communication between the physical and spiritual selves. If you find yourself in an indecisive state, don't compound the problem with worry. Instead, explain the situation to your spiritual self. Wait for an answer and take its advice. It's the only way to break the chains that bind you, and gain the personal freedom you deserve.

Eight of Swords

Characters: Rip Van Winkle and his dog
Story: Rip Van Winkle

Eight of Swords

Description:

Rip Van Winkle was a likable sort. No matter what happened, he was always there when someone needed a helping hand. He fixed fences, located stray cattle, and came up with solutions to seemingly impossible situations. He even went as far as to invent things to make life easier for his neighbors.

Rip's only flaw was that he never tended to his own belongings. He seemed oblivious to the fact that his house was falling down around his ears, that his fences were in ill-repair, or that his livestock was wandering off. He never noticed that his wife needed help or that his children needed support. Instead, he just helped the neighbors, then meandered through the woods to hunt and dream.

In this depiction, Rip lies dreaming on the forest floor while the world goes on without him. He's been missing for so many years that everyone thinks he's dead. His dog knows better, though, and does her best to wake him. What will he find when he opens his eyes? What lessons will finally become clear?

Advice:

When the Eight of Swords creeps into your spread, it's time to stop daydreaming and take a good look at what's going on around you. Up to this point, you haven't been able to see the forest for the trees. Idealism isn't a luxury you can afford right now. Wake up. A reality check is in order.

Take off the rose-colored glasses this instant. They'll only make things worse. Whether you like it or not, you live in the real world, and real problems are screaming for your attention. If you brush them aside, they'll only get worse. Tend to them now, or it may be too late.

Scrutinize each problem thoroughly and completely. Explore your options. Solutions are there; you just have to open your eyes and see them. Once you do, take action. Rectify each malady in its entirety now, and you won't have to deal with it again.

Then take measures against your tendency to drift off to fantasy land again. Remember that your love for dreaming is what got you in this mess. Make a concerted effort to see things as they really are, and tend to problems as they arise. If you do, real life will become much more fun. In fact, you may never crave the dream world again!

Seven of Swords

Character: The Knave of Hearts
Nursery Rhyme: The Knave of Hearts

Description:

The Knave of Hearts doesn't lack intelligence. A member of the royal family, he's been educated by the best teachers that money could buy. Neither is he lacking in skills. He's been trained to fence and fight. He understands business strategy and knows how to rule countries. He's even got a bit of black-smithing, horticulture, and falconry under his belt. But for all of that, he has a problem. Simply put, the Knave of Hearts is lazy. Instead of applying himself toward honest work and reward, he spends his time figuring out ways to get what he wants with little or no effort.

Here we see the Knave of Hearts in action. He sneaks along, staying close to the ground and making sure that no one sees him. Then he steals the tarts left cooling on the windowsill. He had enough money to pay for them. The cook probably would have given them to him freely, if he'd just had the common decency to ask. That was too much trouble for the Knave, though. He's just what his title implies, a good-for-nothing thief.

Advice:

If the Seven of Swords steals into your spread, chances are there's a thief on the loose, and he may be eyeing your valuables. Take inventory of your material possessions and check for missing items. If everything's there, take precautions to prevent future loss. Put valuable items in a safe place, then check to make sure that all windows and doors are locked. It might even be a good time to install that security system you've been thinking about.

Sometimes, this card also indicates that someone is trying to take something much more important than your material possessions. While it could be the commitment of a friend or a love interest, it's more likely that the merchandise in question is a piece of yourself. For that reason, take steps not to lose yourself in any relationship. Take stock of what makes you the person that you are—the personal characteristics that make you an individual—and what sets you apart from everyone else in the world. Then hold tight to those things, as well as your personal code of ethics. Afterward, if you feel certain personal attitudes or perceptions need adjustment, so be it. Just don't change to suit someone else. What's sure to follow will definitely be more than you imagined.

Six of Swords

Characters: Wynken, Blynken, and Nod
Nursery Rhyme: Wynken, Blynken, and Nod

Six of Swords

Description:

Wynken, Blynken, and Nod were just like most other children. Going to bed was not in their plans. They thought all the fun would stop if they closed their eyes, and then they just might miss something important. They had no way of knowing that the world of sleep and dreams held a great amount of magic. It could lead them to wondrous and exciting adventures, to places impossible to reach from the mundane world, or tell them stories that they couldn't hear on any other plane.

Here we see the friends on a sea-faring journey through the night sky. Their vessel of choice, a wooden shoe, is a product of the earth that guarantees their safe passage. Their net of silver and gold symbolizes the strong connection between the spiritual and physical worlds. The Moon Goddess watches over them from above, and gives direction as necessary. She also advises them where to cast their nets to catch the most fish, for they represent valuable lessons to take back with them as they sail toward home.

Advice:

When the Six of Swords sails into a spread, it's time to pay attention to your dreams. They are the key to your spiritual side, a part of yourself that's been ignored much too long. With that in mind, keep a piece of paper and pen next to your bed. Then, after rising each morning, record every dream detail you can remember. If you're well-versed in dream interpretation, you'll know what the symbols mean. If not, treat yourself to a dream dictionary. Analyzing your dream messages will not only aid you on the inner journey, but will also bring you much closer to the completion of your spiritual transformation.

Often, this card is also a signal to temporarily break free of the rat race, and to sort things through. Listen to your inner voice. Not the one in your head, but the one that lies deep down inside you. It's the voice of gut instinct, the voice that commandeers all emotions and feeling. The advice is always there, and the message is loud and clear. Pay attention, and you will learn what to keep and what to throw out. Don't stop there, though. Heed every smidgen of advice your inner voice offers. Your life will be much richer for the balance.

Five of Swords

Characters: The Pied Piper, the children
and the townsfolk
Story: The Pied Piper of Hamelin

Five of Swords

Description:

It all started with a broken contract. Had the villagers paid
the Piper as agreed, life might have gone on undisturbed. Such
was not the case, however. Greed got in the way. Common sense
flew out the window. Arrogance slithered in and reared its ugly
head. Before long, the high and mighty villagers no longer cared
about the importance of honesty and integrity, or the power of
promises rendered. They were so wrapped up in themselves that
they completely underestimated the Piper, and because of that,
life as they knew it ceased to exist.

Here we see the Piper happily leading a parade. He skips through town, playing a lilting, merry melody. The village children dance and laugh as they follow in his steps. Not everyone is enjoying the fun, though. Shock and horror lines the faces of those who look on. They simply cannot believe that the Piper is stealing their children. Even worse, they don't know how to stop him. Perhaps they should just pay him. But no one in this depiction offers a single farthing.

Advice:

The appearance of the Five of Swords in a spread usually indicates that it's time to pay the piper. While this expense might take any form, the toll is most likely personal, rather than financial. It may be time to return a favor or keep your word. It may be time to admit a mistake. It could even mean that an apology is in order.

Don't worry that the nature of your personal fee might be unclear. It won't be. What's more, you'll know precisely when payment is due. Don't delay. Pay the cost, whatever it is, and pay it on time. This is very important because it's possible that the price you owe may not be a comfortable one. It may involve taking a good hard look at your personal imperfections, or something else just as distasteful. That being the case, it will be much easier to handle if you simply step forward and get it done. Any delay will only cause increased personal stress and anxiety.

In the future, take time to look at the big picture before making a decision that puts your neck on the line. Examine each facet carefully and thoroughly. In doing so, you'll be less likely to cut off your nose to spite your face. Understand that you may still lose a battle, but you definitely won't lose the war.

Four of Swords

Character: The Princess
Story: The Princess and the Pea

Four of Swords

Description:

When the Princess climbed to the top of her billowy feather bed, it never occurred to her that a trick was in the works. She'd had a very long day. The journey was not only exhausting, but filled with little aggravations every step of the way. All she could think about was curling up on a soft cloud of feathers, and giving herself totally and completely to the dream world.

It didn't happen. Here we see the Princess fluffing her pillow in despair. Try as she might, she just can't find a comfort zone. She's counted sheep. She's counted suitors. She's even gone as far as to count the fringes on her canopy. Yet there she lies, tossing and turning, even after such an exhausting day.

If the Princess weren't so tired, she might realize that counting games won't help. It might occur to her that she has a real problem that won't just go away by itself. Of course, that would take some effort on her part. She'd have to shinny down the ladder and take a peek, then take some action to resolve it.

Advice:

When the Four of Swords bursts through a spread, it's telling you that the time for rest and relaxation has come. The message slices through the Cosmos with perfect clarity. It says you need rest. It says you need relaxation. Moreover, it says if you don't get some of each real soon, a severe health problem could be at hand.

More than likely, worry is the culprit. Understand that worry is not the same as sorting through things to solve a problem. It is a needless, bothersome emotion that—if fed and left to its own devices—can literally wrench the life from you. Keeping that in mind, learn to slam your emotional doors every time it comes to call. Worry hates that, and will soon find someone else to bother.

What if you still can't rest? Take a deep breath, and close your eyes. Let a smile cross your lips. Visualize a place that's calm and peaceful, a place where no trouble, misery, or paranoia can enter. See yourself kicking back by the ocean. Feel the caress of the sea breezes upon your face. Hear the kiss of the ocean waves on the shore. You'll be asleep before you know it!

Three of Swords

Characters: Hansel and Gretel
Story: Hansel and Gretel

Three of Swords

Description:

When Hansel and Gretel set out to explore the forest, they had no idea that anything bad might happen to them. They were, after all, prepared. Since there is safety in numbers, they stayed together. They brought some lunch to quench their hunger. And just in case they got lost, they'd planned to sprinkle a bread crumb trail behind them. They'd considered all the possibilities and covered every base. That being the case, Hansel and Gretel excitedly set off for the adventure of a lifetime.

The children we see here, though, aren't so happy. They are lost, frightened, and crying. It seems they overlooked one very important fact: birds like bread, too. The trail that they so carefully laid for home is just a memory, for the forest birds have been busy gobbling it up. It's getting dark and all the forest trails look the same. They don't have a clue as to what path to take or which way to turn. Life as they know it has ceased to exist.

Advice:

Should the Three of Swords pierce your spread, get out the box of tissues. Heartbreak (in some shape, fashion, or form) is on its way, and soon you'll probably feel like having a good, long cry.

While the appearance of this card often denotes the end of a relationship, it can also signify the close of some important phase in your life. Chances are, this change will be of definite benefit to your future. You won't see it that way at the onset, though. In fact, you'll be very angry at yourself because you didn't see it coming. Take steps to get over it. Do whatever is necessary. Yell and scream. Weep and sob. Throw things if you have to. Just get past the hurt. It's the only way to get on with the future.

Once you've put the past behind you, take on a new attitude. Look at situations before you get involved. See how they will affect you in the long run. If things don't look good, back off while there's still time. Understand that others aren't always as concerned about you as you are about them. Instead of leaving the job to someone else, take the time to tend to your own needs. Exercise a bit of caution, take responsibility for yourself, and you'll always come out ahead.

Two of Swords

Characters: Hansel and Gretel
Story: Hansel and Gretel

Two of Swords

Description:

Life had become grim for Hansel and Gretel since the day they'd stumbled into the Gingerbread House. They had no sense of time, and one day ran into the next. They couldn't run and play like normal children. Fun and laughter were things of the past. Life wasn't even life anymore. It was a dark and gloomy cloud that hung over them with a great measure of uncertainty. Of course, that was before they took action!

Here we see Hansel and Gretel doing just that. Regardless of their lack of physical activity, they've taken some time to exercise their brains. It's finally occurred to them that escape is not an effort in futility, but a real possibility. Working as a team, they've managed to outsmart their evil captor and send her to a speedy end that is so permanent, she'll never be able to hurt anyone ever again.

We look on as smoke billows from the oven. Hansel and Gretel walk away happily. They know now that nothing is beyond their reach, not even the path toward home.

Advice:

Should the Two of Swords drop into your spread, gather your strength and wits about you. The problem at hand isn't nearly as hopeless as you think. All you need to do is clear your mind, evaluate your options, and take the initiative toward finding a remedy.

Don't waste valuable time playing games. Mental juggling acts seldom breed anything more than fear and worry, and you've already had enough of that. Instead, use your head. Look at the facts. This is no time to sugar-coat anything, so be brutally honest about your situation and how you came to be there. Carefully weigh the facts—no matter how hard or cold they are—against every available option to come up with a beneficial solution.

Understand that there is no set of circumstances so tangled that it can't be rectified. More to the point, there is no situation that can't be turned around to your benefit. Sometimes, however, it takes a bit of creative thinking, a pinch of skillful maneuvering, and a touch of tactical strategy. Give it a whirl, and you're likely to come out of this smelling like the proverbial rose!

Ace of Swords

Depiction: A mighty sword

Ace of Swords

Description:

The Ace of Swords is, perhaps, the most aggressive card in the Tarot. That's because it speaks of strength, courage, and victory. It drives home the importance of the ability to stand up for what we believe in, and the other things that we, as humankind, hope are in our power to accomplish. For this reason, it is always shown as a sharp, double-edged blade—the standard weapon of choice in many ancient wars.

As symbolized by the dragon's head hilt, this particular blade is one of ferocity and experience. It knows what it is to go to war, fight courageously, and return. It knows the glory of winning, and power and freedom of victory. But it also knows the pain of defeat and has experienced the darkness of poor planning. All of this makes for a very balanced blade.

The Moon phases engraved upon the blade represent the blessing of the Goddess, and the ribbons that flow freely from the hilt remind us that creative maneuvering during battle is often in order. But what of the thorny roses? They keep us ever mindful that while freedom is beautiful and sweet smelling, there is always a price to pay—and sometimes, we have to pay for it in blood.

Advice:

When the Ace of Swords slices through your spread, get out the laurel wreath and prepare a speech. You have gained strength and earned power. And now it's time to claim your victory. This is not some small victory, as hinted at by other cards. For you, this specific event is huge. It is a turning point in your life, a day that you will always remember. It commemorates a time when you took up a cause, fought courageously for its principles, and won against all odds.

So, go ahead. Take a bow. Let out a rebel yell. Dance the victory dance, then pat yourself on the back. You deserve it. During your celebration, though, remember what it takes to be a good winner. Give some thought to your opponent. A note or a few words regarding a battle well-fought may be in order.

Remember, too, that the Ace of Swords is not only razor sharp and bears a double-edge, but is much heavier than its counterpart, the fencing blade. Understand that a great amount of strength is necessary to wield it with grace and honor. With that in mind, make sure you are up to the task before you grab its hilt. If you are, it will always serve you well. If not, you may just slip and cut your own throat.

The Suit of Rods

Rods belong to the element of Air, and signify its force at work in our lives. Our physical dependency on Air doesn't end with the human breathing process; we rely on it for benefits we seldom think about. Air controls the breezes that cool the Sun's overpowering heat, and the winds that carry seed pods to the waiting soil. It brings us sound, controls our sense of smell, and to a small degree, our sense of taste. In the abstract, we depend upon this substance for many other things. Thought, communication, inspiration, and ideas fall into its realm, as well as creativity, change, and fresh perspective.

Rods represent fresh starts, beginnings, activity, and the growth necessary for a productive life. Rods clear life's tunnel of darkness, so we can see where we're going and stay on the right track. They give us hope for the future, and prepare us for the beneficial changes life has in store for us. A spread comprised of many Rods signifies a flurry of excitement, change, and activity.

The borders of variegated English ivy on the lesser cards in this suit symbolize the various ways our hopes, dreams, and perspectives change as we travel through life. They remind us to apply our wealth of creative powers toward growth and self-improvement.

✿ ✿ ✿

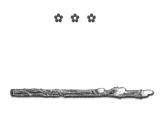

King of Rods

Character: Prince Charming
Story: Cinderella

King of Rods

Description:

Prince Charming is a man of action. He knows what he wants, and leaves no foot in question (as a match for the glass slipper, of course) to get it. Thus, he rules the Suit of Rods and has dominion over inspiration, new beginnings, and fierce determination. The creatures of the Air are drawn to him. Perhaps it's because he wears yellow and green (the colors most often associated with creativity and growth), or maybe it's just that he's so at ease with all of Nature that the creatures can't help but hover around.

The King of Rods is a family man who has a strict set of personal values. But that doesn't mean he's dull or boring. He loves an adventure, walks on the edge, and has a zest for life that's unsurpassed. His most endearing quality, however, is his charming, charismatic manner. Everyone loves him, but what's not to love? He epitomizes the best of both worlds—the stability of reality and the fantasy of the dream world—and in doing so, brings us to the realization that we can have it all, and can be anything we wish.

Advice:

When the King of Rods zips into your spread, it's time to stretch your creative capacity and re-evaluate your personal potential. Wake up and get busy. The time for dreaming is over. While you waste time dreaming of your goals, someone else is achieving them. You can do or be anything you want. All you have to do is decide what you want, reach out, and grab it.

When challenges come to call, show a little enthusiasm. There is nothing too difficult for you to master. You have what it takes to handle whatever is set in front of you. All you need now is a bit of ambition. Look at your goals and think about what it takes to get them. Study your options, then follow through. If you don't see an immediate solution, rely on personal creativity. It will enhance your odds.

The appearance of the King of Rods in a spread can also denote the arrival of a man in your personal life. If that's the case, count yourself lucky. Not only a stable self-starter who delights in holding a job, this person is also fun to be around. His enthusiasm for day-to-day living is infectious, and his personal idea pool is limitless. This man has the best sense of humor of all the Kings in the deck, and the ability to find a bit of joy in even the most dire of situations. Welcome him with open arms. You'll be glad you did.

Queen of Rods

Character: Cinderella
Story: Cinderella

Queen of Rods

Description:

Cinderella rules as the Queen of Rods, and rightly so. No matter how dire her circumstances or how horrible her treatment, she never let it get her down. She just kept on working, kept on smiling, and kept on with the business of living. In the end, she prevailed and won her heart's desire: a charming prince with a gentle heart, a fast horse, and all the love she could ask.

Dressed in the yellow and green of creative growth, the Queen of Rods is the eternal cheerleader. She loves everyone and everything. No matter how difficult the situation, she searches for the silver lining in every storm cloud, then proudly points it out to everyone she sees. Her smile opens doors, her laughter is contagious, and her positive attitude sets a good example for all fortunate enough to know her.

But there's more to the Queen of Rods than a smiling face. A born nester, she's an active domestic goddess and an excellent mother. She nurtures young and old alike. She understands exactly what they need, then takes the action necessary to make their dreams come true.

Advice:

Should the Queen of Rods waltz into your spread, it's time to get off the pity pot. Depression is not only a dead-end street, it breeds anxiety and stress. Left to its own devices, it can even rob you of good health. Instead of dwelling on what's wrong with your life, concentrate on your blessings. Toss away negative feelings and get rid of the pessimistic attitude. Learn to speak in positives rather than negatives. Remove words like "don't," "won't," and "can't" from your vocabulary. After a while, you won't even remember what triggered your initial bout of depression.

Put on a happy front, even if you don't feel like it. Smile. Laugh. Quicken your step. Look for the good in every person and situation. Worried that pretending to be happy is dishonest? Don't be. It's not a crime to trick your brain into thinking you're a cheerful person. Once it believes you are, you will be.

Allow your natural nurturing instincts to surface and help other people with their problems. There's nothing like dealing with the woes of others to make you see how fortunate you are. Spread a little sunshine. Offer a hug or two. Inspire others to find the happiness life has to offer. The positive energy returned will bring the thrill of true joy to your personal life.

Knight of Rods

Character: Jack
Nursery Rhyme: Jack Be Nimble

Description:

An active boy, Jack is the Knight of Rods personified. He's blessed with a constant flow of both physical and mental energies. And though his mind and body run full speed ahead, Jack never misses anything. The sunflower in his pocket—a symbol of success and good fortune—denotes that he's lucky, too. Because of this, Jack always reaches his goals. He knows that the key to success lies in taking action. He never hesitates. He just gets on with things.

In this depiction, we see Jack in mid-air, jumping high over the candle stick. He doesn't worry about falling, for he is nimble. He doesn't worry that his clothes will catch fire, either. He is, after all, quick. In fact, Jack worries very little about anything that life deals him. He knows that he can get through whatever comes his way. All he has to do is jump high and run fast. And Jack can do that with ease. He is the Prince of Activity, a taker of chances, and a real mover and shaker.

Advice:

If the Knight of Rods bursts into your spread, expect a flurry of activity to enter your life. Back-burner projects suddenly move to the foreground. Influential people come into play. Your dreams are now only one step away from reality. All you have to do is get off your duff and take action. Voice your opinions, ideas, and personal philosophies without fear of rejection. This time, they'll be met with the interest and attention they deserve.

The days of playing it safe are over. Take a chance. Force yourself to be spontaneous by making a few last minute decisions. Throw inhibitions aside, and explore uncharted waters. Do something you've always wanted to do. Your creative flow is at an all-time high right now. Jot down project ideas; then go to work on the one that seems the most fun. Don't worry that someone might think it silly or meaningless. It's time to seize the day.

Physical energy is abundant now, too. Use this period to work out a daily exercise program. Doing so will insure against a sluggish attitude and poor health down the road. Run. Jump. Work off some of that excess energy. Not only will you feel better, it will also clear your mind of any clutter that could plug up your creative energy flow later.

Page of Rods

Depiction: A royal page

Page of Rods

Description:

In medieval times, the blowing of a horn was an important event. It's sharp, clear melody signaled the townsfolk to drop whatever they were doing and run quickly toward the sound. It heralded the coming of an announcement by the royal page. Sometimes it was a declaration of war. On other occasions, a party invitation. At any rate, the sounding of the horn always marked an announcement of great significance, a message that might change their lives, something they couldn't afford to miss.

Here we see the page's horn all dressed up in royal splendor. It's sound has gotten our attention. Ribbons twirl gaily in the breeze. A velvet-lined parchment unfurls complete with the message to be delivered. We hurriedly scan the announcement, but can't quite make out wording. It's just too small to read. We'll have to wait patiently for the page to speak, and we must remember to pay attention, too. For it's certain that the words he utters will bring great changes to life as we know it.

Advice:

Because the Page of Rods is the harbinger of important communications, his appearance in a spread always brings a multitude of phone calls, announcements, and assorted messages. Still your mind and listen carefully. Personal messages from your Spiritual Self are likely to arrive now, too. Heed whatever advice is offered. These communications (both mundane and spiritual) are likely to change life as you know it into something more positive and thrilling than you could ever imagine.

You may hear from people you haven't spoken to in awhile, and old friends may suddenly turn up on your doorstep. Don't be surprised if they bring their children. Be warm. Be friendly. Welcome them with open arms and extend some old-fashioned hospitality. Their reappearance in your life is a sign of synchronicity at work. They are there to play a strategic role in the Ancient's plans to better your life.

The appearance of the Page of Rods also signals a good time to move forward with home, business, or real estate projects. Acquire property. Draw up plans. Build, remodel, and renovate. Breathe new life and charm into something old and decrepit. The part you play in its rebirth will, in many ways, bring about your own.

Ten of Rods

Character: The Princess
Story: The Goose Girl

Ten of Rods

Description:

It all started out happily enough. The beautiful princess was on the way to meet her betrothed. Her head was filled with visions of wondrous sights and a lifetime of marital bliss. She just hadn't counted on betrayal, especially not by her lady-in-waiting.

Here we see the princess in the throes of emotional burden, grief, and depression. Her faithful talking horse is dead. Her royal clothing and identification are gone, too (both stolen by her handmaiden). And if that's not bad enough, the wind has stolen the only thing that could save her at this point—a charm made of her mother's handkerchief and blood. The princess sobs pitifully as the charm floats downstream. It's just out of reach, and she can't swim.

Perhaps all is not as dismal as she thinks, though. Several patches of flowers bloom with promise nearby. The sun shines overhead. A raven flies in the direction of the handkerchief. Will he fly on by or swoop down to retrieve it for her?

Advice:

When the Ten of Rods shows up in a spread, flex all emotional muscles and muster every shred of mental strength. Otherwise, you may feel as if the weight of the world is on your shoulders. It's likely that friends and relatives will come to you with their problems right now. They don't want your advice. What they really want is for you to hold their personal bags of garbage for a while. Not wanting to deal with anything unpleasant, they dump problem after problem in your lap, and happily skip off to greener pastures. Coupled with your own problems, the burden gets so heavy that you can't manage it either.

Stop! Don't take another step. Understand that you are not responsible for problems that don't involve you. You played no part in creating these unpleasant circumstances, and it isn't your job to sort them out. This is not to say that you shouldn't offer moral support or a few kind words. However, taking responsibility for other people's problems doesn't do anybody a favor. It not only creates immeasurable stress for you, but teaches others that they don't have to take responsibility for their own actions.

Nine of Rods

Character: Little Boy Blue
Nursery Rhyme: Little Boy Blue

Nine of Rods

Description:

Here we see Little Boy Blue sleeping soundly by the haystack. He has no idea that the animals entrusted to him have meandered into parts unknown. It never occurred to him that they might wander off or get hurt unless he kept a watchful eye. He just assumed that they could take care of themselves. So, the trusting boy settled in for a peaceful nap, quite oblivious to the fact that his world is quickly crumbling around him.

Sadly enough, Little Boy Blue does not understand the need for supervision or the magnitude of that responsibility. After all, the Sun rises and sets, the world spins 'round, and everything always seems to fall into place by natural order. Life goes on, and nothing out of the ordinary ever happens. There's simply nothing to worry about. At least, not in his young life.

Today, however, will bring something new. He will learn that everything is not always as it appears, and that which he cherishes could be lost forever. Once and for all, he will finally understand the importance of paying attention.

Advice:

If the Nine of Rods slips into your spread, be warned that danger—at least in regard to your possessions—is on the loose, and it's headed straight for your door. This may only be a minor mishap instead of a theft, but precautionary measures should be taken to protect what is yours. Now is a good time to secure valuables, lock doors, and keep an eye on your wallet or purse. Check bills carefully. If you're not sure about a particular charge, make a phone call and rectify the matter now. If you wait, it may be too late.

Keep a watchful eye on loved ones, especially children and pets. Confine pets to the house, the yard, or their leashes. If children frequent play areas away from home, ask them to check in at regular intervals. A word of caution about common sense and "stranger danger" might not hurt, either.

Refrain from taking that spur-of-the-moment trip right now. Instead, opt for carefully planned vacations and outings. Double-check bookings and reservations. Pay attention to the weather forecast. Pack extra cash and clothing, check the spare tire for air, and above all, take your time while traveling. Planning for emergencies takes a little extra time, but it's the very best way to ensure a safe and pleasant trip.

Eight of Rods

Nursery Rhyme: Row, Row, Row Your Boat

Eight of Rods

Description:

The scene depicted here is picture perfect. The sun is shining. The waters are calm. The shoreline is bright with the greening of Spring. It's a beautiful day, and all is right with the world. So right, in fact, it's almost like a dream.

The people in the boat are happy and excited. Map in tow, they've set off on a journey, and it's proving to be a real adventure. As they travel downstream, they animatedly discuss their plans. They talk about where they've been, where they're going, and what they'll do when they reach their destination.

In between, they talk about their good fortune, their hopes and dreams for the future, and all that they hold personally important. Their laughter rings out across the water. The gentle breeze picks it up and carries it far off into the distance, communicating their joy to others.

Just as they round the bend, a fairytale castle comes into view. It's well kept and inviting. Have they reached their destination? Or will they go on? We have no way of knowing, for this adventure is theirs alone.

Advice:

Smile when the Eight of Rods floats into your spread, for it brings long distance messages of good luck, good fortune, and happiness. Synchronicity comes into play, bringing many of your hopes and dreams within arm's reach. Suddenly, all that is good in the Cosmos seems focused directly on you. With so much going right in your life, you may feel the need to pinch yourself awake. Don't. It's not a dream. You've waited a lifetime for this moment, and you deserve it. All you have to do now is enjoy it.

Part of the reason life seems to have a dream-like quality right now is because everything is moving so quickly. Communications—especially phone calls, letters, and e-mail—begin to arrive with great frequency. Don't allow yourself to become overwhelmed. Grab a piece of paper, and take some notes. Write down anything you think you might forget. Just knowing that you can refer to your notes later will ease your mind now.

Occasionally, the Eight of Rods also brings an offer of a trip over water. Should that be the case, pack your bags and go. Not only will you have a terrific time, the wonders you'll experience may forever change your life.

Seven of Rods

Characters: Jack and the Giant
Story: Jack and the Beanstalk

Description:

When the Giant killed his father, Jack didn't know what to do. The Giant was big and mean. Jack was small, frail, and obviously no match for such an ogre. All Jack knew was that he had two choices. He could either try to out run the monster, or he could stay and fight. Fortunately for the fairy tale world, Jack chose the latter. Truth be told, he couldn't do anything else. No matter how afraid Jack was, he knew that he had to face his fear. He had to slay the Giant before he hurt anyone else physically or financially. It was the only right thing to do.

In order to accomplish this task, of course, Jack had to take a hefty risk. He had to purposely upset the Giant, come face to face with him, and aggravate him so badly that he couldn't help but race down the beanstalk in the hope of ripping Jack limb from limb. Jack, however, stood firm. He took a deep breath and cleared his mind. Then, he carefully laid out his plans and followed through. When all was said and done, Jack found he'd recovered more than the family fortune. He'd recovered the self-worth and personal confidence he thought was lost forever.

Advice:

Should the Seven of Rods appear in your spread, it's time to stand up for what you believe in. Don't worry about what others think. Everyone has his own path, and what's right for you doesn't have to be right for anyone else. State your case, and stick to your guns. Do whatever it takes to rectify the matter at hand. You know the difference between right and wrong, and the time has come for you to set things straight.

This is not the time to be cajoled into following the crowd or taking the easy way out, especially if it means compromising your personal code of ethics. How you feel about things and how you react to certain situations sets you apart as an individual. It makes you who you are, and to a large degree, who you will become in the future. More importantly, your code of ethics mirrors your personal sense of integrity, which is the only thing that sets you apart as a member of humankind.

Now is the time to face your greatest fear. No matter how daunting it seems, don't hesitate. Gather your courage, and face it head-on. You have the tools necessary to conquer your fear and attain victory. Afterward, you'll be surprised at how little effort it took to accomplish a feat of such magnitude.

Six of Rods

Character: Dorothy
Story: Wizard of Oz

Description:

When the tornado whipped through Kansas, it never occurred to Dorothy that she might not ever see her home or family again. And even if it had, she probably wouldn't have cared. Fact is, she found farm life dull and boring. She longed for some real excitement.

Had she moved away by choice, she might always have felt that way. Instead, she was whisked into a strange, faraway place by a twist of fate. Suddenly, the very life she'd looked upon with disdain gained new importance. It became so important, in fact, that she spent her entire adventure battling wicked witches and all their horrors just to find her home again.

Here we see Dorothy with Toto. A rainbow lights the sky with promise. Eyes closed in concentration, Dorothy firmly clicks her heels together and intones the magical words, "There's no place like home." The battle she's fought so long and hard is finally won. Victory is hers. At last, she's returning to Kansas, to the life and family she once thought so dull.

Advice:

When the Six of Rods marches into your spread, it's time to take a long, deep breath. The scent of victory is in the air, and its perfume belongs to you. The things for which you've worked so hard are yours now. You've finally won the war, and no one can take that away from you.

Take a moment to pat yourself on the back. Do a victory dance. Laugh, sing, and rejoice. Your adversary was tough and formidable. The odds weren't in your favor. Yet, you fought well. You fought fairly. You never once resorted to underhanded tactics to gain leverage against your opponent. Know that this is the most important reason for celebration, for only a very special person can consistently adhere to a code of ethics without regard to personal cost.

Know what it takes to be a good winner, then follow through. Once you've learned to be kind, generous, and gracious in the face of victory, your success is matched with respect. Understand that true victory is much more than winning the game or using perfect strategy. It's the way you behave at the awards ceremony that really tells the tale.

Five of Rods

Characters: Brer Rabbit and the Tar Baby
Story: Brer Rabbit and the Tar Baby

[Tales from Uncle Remus]

Five of Rods

Description:

While Brer Rabbit was a likable sort, his constant chatter presented a problem. Even worse, he couldn't mind his own business. It wasn't that he had no personal business to tend. It was just so much more fun to interfere in everyone else's. Brer Fox finally had enough. He devised a plan to put Brer Rabbit in his place, once and for all.

Here we see Brer Rabbit with the Tar Baby. Angry because the tar figure refused to speak to him or answer his questions, he finally took a poke at it. An awful struggle ensued. First, his hand got stuck. The more he pulled, the faster it stuck. And the faster it stuck, the more angry he became. Infuriated, Brer Rabbit punched the Tar Baby with the other fist, then gave it a swift kick. The results were the same. Before it was said and done, the nosy, noisy rabbit was not only covered in tar, but had lost his pride and dignity—something that might have been prevented had he gone along his merry way and simply minded his own business.

Advice:

When the Five of Rods marches into your spread, gather your ammunition, and throw up your shields. A fight or struggle is in the works, and trouble is on the way. It's time for you to gather a plan of action, and take a firm stand. Know that this struggle isn't always physical. More often, it takes the form of an emotional dilemma that stems from confusion, and from not knowing how to respond to a particular set of circumstances. Confusion breeds worry, and worry breeds stress. For that reason, don't spend a lot of time and energy juggling between what's right and wrong. Take a deep breath or two, and clear your head. Then, follow the first course of action that pops into your head.

Sometimes this card also foretells unforeseen trouble or things getting in the way of important plans. If that's the case, just go with the flow. Know that change, while sometimes aggravating or painful, is always a good thing. Sometimes, it's just hard for us to see the big picture. Understand that the Cosmic forces always have your best interest at heart, no matter what annoyances have crossed your path.

Four of Rods

Scene: A fairy tale castle

Four of Rods

Description:

Who wants to live in a castle? Nearly every child on Earth! Though reasons vary, all agree that these structures give off an air of wonder, excitement, and wealth. Born of every small child's fantasy, the regal building depicted here is definitely a sanctuary. The outer walls are strong. They keep intruders at bay, and ensure that those who live inside are safe and secure.

We can tell that this castle is more than a safe haven, though. It's a happy home. The grounds are neatly groomed, well-kept, and cared for. The cobblestone walkway is clean and free of debris. Castle walls and turrets wear a fresh coat of paint.

Even so, there are much larger clues that reveal a peaceful and loving existence here. Flowers thrive across the stream nearby. The red turrets (symbolizing love) are festooned with garlands fashioned from their blossoms and hung with the utmost care. The bluebirds of happiness fly overhead, bringing their own sort of magic to rest—the final flowering garland that completes our vision of the harmony which exists inside.

Advice:

The Four of Rods is a fortunate card for everyone, but is especially significant for those who have been plagued with a chaotic home-life. The peace and happiness you've dreamed of is now waiting for you. All you have to do is open the door and walk in.

The Cosmos has just cleaned house. Gone are the days of disharmony, argumentative behavior, and sadness. Gone are the days of worry and stress. Negative vibrations and feelings of unease have been swept away as well. The whole environment has been cleansed with positive, loving energy. All that's left is a protected atmosphere where positive characteristics and virtues can grow and thrive.

That being the case, do your best to keep negative energy at bay. How? Never bring worries, work, or problems home with you. Don't brood. Instead, keep things light and happy. Laugh, love, and have fun. Fill your life to the brim with tender loving care, and it will always be the sanctuary you desire and deserve.

In the case of those looking for a change of residence, this card often signifies that your dream home is now within grasp. Consult the newspaper or contact your real estate agent today.

Three of Rods

Characters: The townsfolk and the visitors
Story: Stone Soup

Three of Rods

Description:

It all started when a trio of penniless travelers hit town. Though they were tired and in need of a bath, their biggest problem went much deeper. They hadn't eaten in days, and were more than a little hungry. They were positively ravenous. With no money in their pockets, though, what were they to do?

Despite their grumbling bellies, one of the travelers sat down to think. Before long, they'd come up with the perfect solution. It was a solution so perfect, that the whole town cheerfully joined in to feed them.

Here we see teamwork at its best. Townsfolk come from far and wide bringing whatever they can spare from their cupboards (a potato here, a carrot there, a bowl of turnips, corn, and squashes). Those who can't spare food help in other ways. They kindle the fire. They stir the pot. They keep the travelers from adding too many stones. Each one contributes to the project at hand, and before long, their efforts bring the desired results: a delicious, hearty culinary delight. And all it took was a little teamwork and a few stones.

Advice:

When the Three of Rods sweeps into your spread, it's time to flex creative muscles. Gather ideas. Sort through them one at a time, then glue them together and set them into motion. If some ideas don't fit your current purpose, don't discard them as silly or frivolous. Know that what may not seem like a good idea now may be the beginning of something wonderful later.

If you can't get a project to come together on your own, bend some ears. Use friends as a sounding board. Listen to what they have to say. Consider their questions and advice. Because they're more likely to view things objectively, they may see ready solutions to problem areas or come up with ideas that will improve the project as a whole.

Remember that teamwork is often the reason that creative ideas and endeavors manifest into reality. Take the Seven Wonders of the World, for example. No one single-handedly brought them into existence. It took many heads, many hands, and many back-breaking hours to bring them to fruition. Be that as it may, however, they all began as one idea that formed in someone's head. Recognize that the same may be true of your project, and that you may need help to bring about the results you desire.

Two of Rods

Character: The Lion and the Mouse
Story: The Lion and the Mouse
[Aesop's Fables]

Two of Rods

Description:

Since the beginning of time, lions have been known for their size, strength, courage, and stability. Mice, however, aren't known for any of those characteristics. They seem small and trivial by comparison. In fact, they are generally thought of as nothing more than a nuisance. Here, however, we gain new insight into the mouse's character.

In this depiction, the lion struggles endlessly to break free of the net. He growls, roars, and thrashes about; but no matter how fierce his efforts, he only serves to entangle himself further. For all practical purposes, further efforts promise futility. The lion's personal freedom is lost.

The mouse, though, has talents that the lion does not; qualities like razor sharp teeth, tenacity, and a stubborn streak a mile wide. He also has a good memory, and knows that one good turn deserves another. For these reasons, he comes to the aid of his friend. He patiently chews through each strand of netting. Soon, the lion will be free to roam once more and reclaim his title as King of the Jungle.

Advice:

If the Two of Rods pops up in your spread, kick back and breathe a sigh of relief. Your problems are over, for Cosmic solutions are at hand. They just may not come in the forms you expect. That being the case, pay close attention to the things going on in your world. Listen to bits and pieces of conversations as they fly past. Don't worry that it's rude to eavesdrop. It's possible that a word or phrase spoken to another might prompt a solution. Pay close attention to your dreams, too, and write them down while they're still fresh in your mind. If you don't understand their messages, consult a dream dictionary. This is important because dream messages often bring new perception, and reveal situational angles previously ignored.

Help may also come from friends and relatives as well as strangers. But know that the solution may not come in words. It may come in the form of an opportunity, a gift, or simply by watching the behavioral patterns of others and studying their reactions. The form it takes is not important. Understand that higher powers are cheering you on, and will provide you with whatever you need to handle the problems at hand.

Ace of Rods

Depiction: A walking staff

Description:

The Ace of Rods is a wondrous card, signaling the birth of self-growth, inspiration, creativity, and fresh starts. Here we see a depiction of a walking staff capped with a crystal ball. The gnarled piece of wood symbolizes the twists and turns we take through life to reach our goals; while the crystal ball signifies the human ability to envision our future and determine personal destiny. Newly sprouted variegated ivy twirls around the staff, pushing its roots deep into its crevices and finally resting gracefully atop the crystal orb. The ivy promises the beauty of growth with each step we take and each decision we make while on the personal path. The moon phases on the staff remind us that the God/dess is always close by to offer help and assistance should we falter along the way.

A wreath of daisies and black-eyed susans frame the crystal ball, and butterflies flit here and there. The flowers represent creativity at maturity, and the balance of dark and light necessary to complete such growth. Like the butterfly, we must have the courage to leave what is safe and venture into unknown areas. Once we achieve personal metamorphosis and drink the nectar of creativity, we can tie up life's loose ends—much like the loops of the bow shown in this card.

Advice:

When the Ace of Rods blossoms in your spread, get ready for a sudden burst of creativity, inspiration, and a boundless amount of energy. Welcome the sprouting and budding of a fresh, new start. Open your eyes. See the opportunities that await you. Open your mind, and look deep within the crystal ball. Grab what life has to offer, and sample it all. Take a few chances. After all, the Fates are smiling upon you now.

Find new ways to express yourself creatively. Do something impulsive. Twirl in the wind, toast the sun, dance in the rain, hug a tree. Feel the power of Nature surge through your center and revitalize the creative powers sleeping deep inside. Start new projects. Let go of the old ideas that held you back and follow your whims. If you don't like your life or who you've become, now is the time to change it. You have the power to be anyone you want to be.

Plant, water, and fertilize the seeds of self-growth. Learn something new. Enthusiastically master that which challenges you. Widen your circle of friends and rekindle old relationships. Learn from past mistakes and start life anew. Fully embrace rebirth, and accept your personal metamorphosis.

The Suit of Cups

Cups symbolize the element of Water in our lives. Water flows, shrinks, cools, cleanses, and stagnates. It manifests in various forms—mist, rain, tears, dew, seafoam—and each is important to our world. It is commonly known as the life-giving element, for without it, humankind would cease to exist.

The Moon rules this essential substance, just as it rules our hearts and emotions. Therefore, cups signify emotional response and form the heart of the Tarot. Whether happy and romantic, or sad and remorseful, they mirror our feelings and give them credence. A spread comprised of many cups generally signifies joy.

The blue morning glories that border the cards of this suit symbolize the necessity of both water and emotion as we wander through life. The twisting, twining vines and heart-shaped leaves remind us of the hairpin curves that emotion can take in our lives. They also prompt us to remember that sure footing and a slow pace make for good progress along the personal path.

King of Cups

Character: King Arthur
Story: Camelot/King Arthur and
the Knights of the Round Table

King of Cups

Description:

Arthur, the King of Cups, rules love and human sensitivity. With his Queen, he has co-dominion with over the Moon, Sea, and emotional response. He wears the soothing colors of the ocean, and opens his arms wide to embrace all that its life-giving waters offer.

The King of Cups is a gentle man, who is always sensitive to the needs of those around him. He is good-hearted, protective, and loving. This makes him an excellent friend and the perfect choice for an intimate relationship. He loves people, and is often found in party situations.

The King's only flaw is that he often has difficulty saying what he means, and meaning what he says. But he is not a liar, a schemer, or a troublemaker. He understands first-hand what it is to be hurt, and absolutely refuses to offer that sort of pain to anyone else. For this reason, he often avoids issues entirely, or makes a practice of not telling the whole truth. Rather than a lack of honesty, love, or honor, his flaw comes from the sensitivity of human nature.

Occasionally, the King of Cups represents a good-hearted person with a substance abuse problem. If that's the case, know that his inability to handle alcohol or drugs stems from the pain of those around him. When they find happiness, he usually finds the strength to stop abusing himself and becomes, again, the wonderful man that he really is.

Advice:

When the King of Cups meanders through a spread, it's time to step outside yourself and look closely at the needs of others. Let your gentle nature take over, and allow sensitivity to be your guide. Take loved ones by the hand, let them know you're there for them. Offer a strong shoulder to cry on, even if it tests your patience.

Although life includes unpleasant events, dealing with them is necessary for spiritual lesson-learning. The success of others depends upon your honesty. Help them deal with circumstances in a straightforward manner, and temper any criticism with plenty of hugs and a healthy dose of kindness. Remember that the seriousness of any circumstance can be diffused with humor. Give laughter a whirl. It provides the ammunition necessary to put one foot in front of the other as we walk the path of life.

Queen of Cups

Character: Guinevere
Story: Camelot/King Arthur and
the Knights of the Round Table

Queen of Cups

Description:

Guinevere, the Queen of Cups, co-rules the Moon, the Sea and emotions. She wears a blue-green gown and her hair is adorned with the treasured gifts of the ocean. She holds the goblet of love high in a toast to the sea and its life-giving waters.

The Queen of Cups is a romantic sort, and as a result, she sees beauty everywhere she looks. Don't mistake her romanticism for air-headedness, though. Her road has been trodden with laughter and tears, smiles and sighs. The joys and heartaches of love belong to her, as well as the emotional roller-coaster of life. She draws upon her wealth of experience to help us understand that real love exists on many levels, and far exceeds our worldly plane.

This lady is a gentle Queen, kind and soft-hearted. She has a sweet, forgiving nature and understands the frailties of humankind. She is a natural mother, nurturing all that cross her path. Her gift is that of unconditional love.

Advice:

When the Queen of Cups graces your spread, it's time to look at life with a loving eye. See the beauty in all that life has to offer—from the yawn of a puppy to the graceful withering of the plant under Winter's harsh frost. Understand that love goes much deeper than hugs and kisses. It requires traveling within and taking inventory of that which makes you an individual. Gather the beauty there, and use it to soften the world's harshness. Make the world a better place with that beauty, and in turn, become the joyful, happy person you were meant to be.

Remember that love is a gentle, kind, and nurturing emotion that carries with it many responsibilities. Get past your old ideas of what love is. Start by learning to accept yourself—getting to know the rise and fall of your emotional tides and your personal imperfections. Then work toward accepting others as they are, too. Be quick to forgive. Realize that love has no terms. Learn to do what is best for other people, regardless of your personal wishes (and if necessary, let them go). Learning to love unconditionally isn't easy, but it's well worth the effort. Its gift, of course, is Divine Love, and that's the greatest love of all.

Knight of Cups

Character: Sir Lancelot
Story: King Arthur and
the Knights of the Round Table

Knight of Cups

Description:

The Knight of Cups is a rare breed. He's a champion, a gentleman, and every little girl's fantasy. Lancelot is indeed such a character. This dashing, handsome charmer has impeccable manners and knows how to use them. His impulsive nature rivals the speed of his horse. And if that's not enough, he holds the cup of spontaneous adventure and romance just within your grasp. Then, he offers it to you.

Here we see Lancelot in glorious splendor. Suited in shining armor with eyes twinkling, he rides tall atop a royal steed. The blue of his cape indicates that his intentions are honorable. But it's his horse who really gives us some insight into what the Knight is thinking. Adorned in the Venusian colors of rose and green, and traveling like the speed of light, the horse heralds his thoughts of romance and the beginning stages of love's whirlwind with all of its celebratory trimmings.

Advice:

When the Knight of Cups rides into your spread, clear your social calendar and prepare for a party. Fun, celebration, and excitement are in the air. Accept phone calls, invitations, and a steady stream of requests for the pleasure of your company. The party has begun, and you are the guest of honor. Smile, laugh, and have fun. Now is not the time for shyness. Forget about your problems and woes. You can always take care of them tomorrow. Take your spot on center stage. Bow, curtsy, and enjoy the spotlight as it shines for you alone.

Love whispers on the wind now, too. Listen carefully. It may call your name. If it does, prepare for flirtation, happy outings, and lots of hand holding. This is a soft and gentle kind of love—the kind that make you feel bubbly, alive, and full of energy. Cast aside fears and hesitation. Don't worry about your heart. Open your arms and embrace it fully. This love knows nothing of the hurt and sorrow that often accompany intimate relationships. It's unconditional, and it knows no boundaries. It is a love song in progress. This is good old-fashioned romance, just the way it was meant to be. What's more, it's yours for the taking. All you have to do is accept it.

Page of Cups
Depiction: A crystal ball

Page of Cups

Description:

The crystal ball is renown for its excellent divination properties. It foretells the future, brings insight to complicated issues, and answers questions with perfect clarity. Before it can help us, though, we must clear our heads of all distractions. We must focus, concentrate, and become one with the ball. As we become one with the ball and travel within, we meet with swirls of brilliant color that wrap us in their kaleidoscopic dance. As we travel deeper, the colors dissipate—slowly at first, then more quickly—until all that's left are the messages we sought to find.

This crystal ball is a very special one. Its sole support comes from the golden fish who live deep in the ocean waters. They remind us that we, too, must travel deep within to find true happiness. They remind us that we must swim to the core of the inner self for perfect clarity and solution. But most importantly, they remind us that we always hold all the answers. We just have to summon the courage to push through the surface and dwell within. Only then will the answers become crystal clear.

Advice:

Should the Page of Cups materialize in your spread, chances are that you're looking for explanations and solutions. You may even feel like you know the answers, but can't get a grip on the questions. Brace yourself. Pack a spiritual bag. Your journey within is about to begin.

As you travel deep inside yourself, take a good look at what makes you the person you are. Some discoveries will be stimulating. Some may make you smile. Others may not be so pleasant, but examine them carefully anyway. The solutions you seek are hiding there somewhere, and you can't afford to miss them.

Know that, in this life, you are never dealt a hand that you can't play; it may just be that you'd rather be holding other cards. There is always a solution to every problem, and the answer lies within you. Think. Meditate. If necessary, call upon your Spirit Guides for help. Ask them to light the way and show you what needs to be seen.

Once a solution becomes apparent, trust yourself enough to follow through. Listen to your head instead of your heart, and take immediate action. Procrastination will only compound matters and present further problems down the road.

Ten of Cups

Characters: Snow White, the Prince, and the Seven Dwarfs
Story: Snow White and the Seven Dwarfs

Description:

The tale of Snow White and the Seven Dwarfs is one of the most beautiful love stories ever told. Here we catch a glimpse of Snow White's new beginning as a queen of distant lands. But it's much more than that. We also get a bird's eye view of the true love and romance shared between Snow White and her prince. Gently lifted into his arms, he carries her through the gilded gates to a new life, a new home, and a new legacy that only comes from the sharing and commitment of married life.

Even though Snow White embarks on a new life with her love, her family still has a place in her life. The dwarfs she so lovingly nurtured and cared for run ahead to explore their new home, and see what delights await them. There, they shall live out their time with the "mother" they adopted so long ago. And so it should be, for true love is much more than mere romance. It is a serious commitment to the lives of each other—lives that should be shared rather than commandeered—so that both may indeed live happily ever after.

Advice:

When the Ten of Cups sweeps into your spread, it's time to say goodbye to romantic flings that end in heartbreak, and say hello to the real thing. The love affair of a lifetime awaits you. It's serious romance, complete with commitment and the legacy of home and family. Even better, it offers the sort of love that can endure growth and change. Like fine wine, this love not only sweetens with age, but also leaves you feeling warm, content, and secure.

The appearance of this card can also signal family members joining together to work toward a common dream or goal, either business or personal. If this is the case, forget everything negative you've ever heard about family members and business. There's nothing to worry about. Destiny smiles on you. This is a successful union that was meant to be. You can't go wrong unless you decide to go it alone.

Open your heart. Take a chance. Worried about commitment? Don't be. Whatever the proposal, this union is solid. You won't be left holding the bag. What's more, love has the capacity to fulfill your deepest hopes and innermost dreams. It's the Cosmos' way of ensuring you the best life has to offer.

Nine of Cups

Character: The Genie
Story: Aladdin's Lamp

Nine of Cups

Description:

The Nine of Cups and the genie who lives inside Aladdin's Lamp have a lot in common. Each has a tremendous amount of magical power. Each has the ability make dreams come true. Most importantly, though, each takes every command seriously and literally. For this reason, wishes must be carefully and specifically worded in order to avoid disappointment or catastrophe.

Here we see the genie materializing as he's called forth from the peaceful depths of his lamp. He grins from ear to ear, a sure sign that he's delighted to be at your service and help you in any way he can. His jewelry is simple, yet costly. It says that no request is too menial or too grand. The fact that he's chubby speaks of abundance, fruitfulness, prosperity, and all it has to offer. He's ready, willing, and waiting. You only have to speak of your desires, and your every wish will be his command.

Advice:

If this card materializes in your spread, you are one of the luckiest people on the planet. Commonly known as the "wish card," the Nine of Cups is the bearer of dreams come true, wishes granted, and Cosmic favors returned. No request is too hefty for the Nine of Cups. It's a little like having a personal genie at your beck and call. You can have anything you want, and it's only a wish away.

Even so, this is no time to be frivolous. Remember the story of the monkey's paw. The wishes were granted, but the route taken toward their fruition was certainly less than desirable. The problem was not with the wishes, but with the lack of specification. You see, the Cosmos is not a reasoning entity. It acts solely on literal thought to achieve an end result. For this reason, be extremely careful what you wish. Give it serious thought and consider any related karmic ramifications. Take the time to specify the events leading up to the results you desire. Roll them over in your mind, and play them out start to finish. If something doesn't feel right, now is the time to make appropriate changes. Once the words are out of your mouth, it may be too late!

Eight of Cups

Character: Little Miss Muffet
Nursery Rhyme: Little Miss Muffet

Eight of Cups

Description:

Sharing breakfast with a spider was not exactly what Little Miss Muffet had in mind when she went outside to eat. Had she stayed indoors, or hadn't been in such a hurry, the problem might have been avoided altogether. The fact is that she just didn't pay attention to what was going on around her. And because of that, she not only created a bad situation for herself, but also managed to leave her breakfast behind.

Here we see Miss Muffet fleeing from the problems of the physical world. The pink of her dress denotes that she must conquer matters close to her heart, emotional matters that can only find resolution on a spiritual level. As she runs toward the safety of her home, it's obvious that mundane matters go on without a hitch. The flowers still bloom. The grass still grows. And the spider—delighted to have something to eat other than insects—continues to travel downward from his web toward the delicacy that awaits. Everything will be as it was when she conquers her fears and returns to the physical realm.

Advice:

When the Eight of Cups rushes into your spread, it's a sign that the hustle and bustle of the physical world is getting to be too much for you. In fact, your physical body may already be telling you to slow down. Exhaustion, mental fatigue, and irritability are some of the clues you might have missed. Still your body. Be quiet and listen carefully to what it has to say. If you don't, you could end up in a sick bed, or even worse.

Now is the time to make a hasty retreat from the craziness of the modern world. Close the windows and lock the doors. Unplug the telephone, turn off the TV, and travel deep within yourself for a bit of rest and regeneration. Your Spiritual Self needs some attention.

The inward journey is often a frightening one; not because we can't let go of the mundane, but because we are unfamiliar with the Spiritual Self. Cast off your fears, relax, and move forward. The Spiritual Self is not only a part of you, it's who you really are! Spend some time getting reacquainted. Talk some, but listen much. Learn about yourself, your place in this life, and the importance of your role in the Cosmic plan. What you discover will forever change the way you view the world and the path you take toward its rewards.

Seven of Cups

Depiction: The roads to the realms of
fairy tales and nursery rhymes

Seven of Cups

Description:

A fork in the road can cause a definite problem, especially
if the routes are unmarked and you don't know where you're
going. Not so with this depiction. The directions for each path
are identified with care. There is no doubt as to their final destination. The only problem here is deciding which road you
wish to travel, and which will bring the most personal benefit.

The road pictured here forks in seven directions, and
offers many possibilities of excitement and adventure. One
road reaches the abundance of the Emerald City; another, the

culinary delights of Gingerbread Lane. Additionally, there are paths to Old McDonald's Farm, the Rabbit Hole, Rapunzel's Tower, and the Market. There's even a path to the Castle of your dreams. Some are rocky. Some are not. Some are straight, and some meander through curves and hills. Which one is best for you? Which route will set you on the most positive personal course? The decision is solely up to you.

Advice:

If the Seven of Cups travels through your spread, clear your mind, and shake off the fog. Options are at hand, and you get to choose. Quickly discard any choice that even hints of negativity. Then focus on each remaining selection carefully and individually. Turn it over in your mind. Look at each facet, angle, and particle. Visualize how a particular option might affect you. Then, think about how it could affect the other people in your life. Since we are strongly connected to those who share our lives, this step is important to personal decision-making. That which affects us also impacts the lives that form our personal network.

But what if there's no right choice? What then? Look again. The choice is there. Perhaps, though, it's an option you'd rather not take. Life is not all sweetness and light. Remember that the Ancients never deal us a hand we cannot play. Gather insight from past experience. Pick the best choice available for all concerned, even if it means choosing between to the lesser of two evils. The direction you choose could affect your life, and the lives of those you love, for quite some time.

Six of Cups

Characters: Peter Pan and Wendy
Story: Peter Pan

Six of Cups

Description:

The innocence of young love is a precious thing. Born of close friendships, fun, and hefty doses of laughter, it's something we never forget. No matter how sad we feel at any given time, we can always conjure it back up. And when we do, it's the one memory in life guaranteed to make us feel better again.

Here we see Peter Pan and Wendy holding hands as they soar above the ocean. They fly high into the blue sky, enjoying the warmth of the sun on their backs. Finally, he looks into her eyes. Then, he offers her a tiny bouquet of flowers that mirror his blossoming feelings for her. Judging by the way Wendy looks back at Peter, we can tell that her feelings for him are growing, too. She loves his strength, his courage, and his sense of adventure. She loves the way he holds her hand, careful to keep her from falling. Most of all, she loves the memory that they creating. Though she understands that age will take her youth, she also knows that the recollection of this precious moment will always keep her young at heart.

Advice:

When the Six of Cups pops into your spread, it generally denotes a repeating of personal history and an opportunity to correct past wrongs. Think about the events of your past and the people connected to them. Look carefully at the episodes which impacted your life in a special way. Pay especially close attention to the ones which didn't turn out so well. If given the chance to re-live them, would you do anything differently? Chances are, you would. With the Cosmos building a bridge between your past and present, that opportunity is coming quickly. This time, though, things can go well. After all, prior experience is on your side.

For that reason, bravely face whatever past-related problems that come your way. Then, go one better by embracing them fully. Know that you now have what it takes to handle the situation, and that you possess the spiritual tools necessary for a beneficial resolution. Take a deep breath and plunge right in! Correcting past errors now will make your future a brighter, smoother, easier place to live.

It's also likely that childhood friends will surface now and re-enter your life. If they do, welcome them back with open arms. Their re-emergence will bring personal pleasure and provide the emotional support necessary for a productive life.

Five of Cups

Character: Captain Hook
Story: Peter Pan

Five of Cups

Description:

The most useless emotion in all of human nature is regret. It keeps us from feeling capable. It keeps us from feeling valuable. But worst of all, it keeps us from counting our blessings and moving on with our lives. Because of this, a much larger problem occurs. We tend to ignore the magic of our world, and miss all the wonders that life has to offer.

Captain Hook is no stranger to regret. In fact, they've been close companions for some time. Late at night, he conjures its presence for a tearful chat. The problem is that Hook cannot get over the loss of his hand. He hates the crocodile and himself, but most of all, he hates the metal contraption that constantly reminds him of his loss. Were it not for all his tears, Hook could see that he has riches beyond compare. He has gold. He has respect. He has all of Never-Never Land to conquer and hold. Yet, he stands there crying, bemoaning the fact that the loss of a single appendage is worth more than all the riches within his grasp. Will he release self-pity and move forward? Only he can decide.

Advice:

When the Five of Cups creeps into your spread, it's a sign that you may have some trouble moving forward with your life. Don't cry over spilled milk or dwell on past mistakes. There's nothing you can do to change the past, the mistakes you've made, or the lives of those you've left behind. What's done is done. Now it's time to mend, discard negative feelings, and move ahead on your path.

This is not to say that you shouldn't remember the circumstances of past mistakes and make corrections as you head towards your personal future. Remember the consequences of those mistakes, and how they have impacted your life. Take special care to avoid current situations that might encourage the same sort of impaired judgment. Treat others as you'd like to be treated—with courtesy, care, and love.

Forgive yourself. You are a good person, but like all of humankind, you have human failings. It's okay not to be perfect. It's okay to make mistakes. Only through human imperfection do you grow strong and wise, both mentally and spiritually. It's a necessary part of your evolution into the person you were born to be.

Four of Cups

Character: The Emperor
Story: The Emperor's New Clothes

Four of Cups

Description:

When the Emperor ordered new clothes, he wanted something more than special. He wanted something extraordinary. He wanted it so badly, in fact, that he began to see things that weren't there. What wasn't there, of course, were his clothes!

Here we see a procession in progress. Knights and guards march through the streets carrying their banners high. The townsfolk run outside to catch a glimpse of the goings-on. Others crane their necks from nearby windows. Some people are shocked. Some feel faint. Some simply can't believe their eyes. It's none other than their beloved ruler atop his favorite steed, and he's parading through town naked as a jaybird! The subjects he approaches do their best to keep straight faces, but those behind him snicker and point. The Emperor is oblivious to that which is obvious to everyone else. And unfortunately, he'll pay for it dearly in the larger scheme of things.

Advice:

Most things in life are of the "what-you-see-is-what-you-get" variety. That is, if it looks like velvet and feels like velvet, it must be velvet. Not so with the Four of Cups. Should this card parade through your spread, take a step back from your situation. Look at it carefully. Roll it over in your mind. Things may not be as they appear, especially if they seem too good to be true. Investigate a little. Scratch the surface. Check for solidity. Stir things up from underneath and see what transpires after the settling. If you don't like what you see now, chances are that you won't like the final outcome, either. Remember, one ill-placed step along the path of life often costs many steps of miserable wandering.

Clarification is the key word here. If you're not sure you understand a request or an offer—particularly one related to a love or business arrangement—ask. If you still aren't sure, ask again. Voice your questions in a straight-forward, direct manner. Now is not the time to worry about looking foolish. The only foolish question is the one left unasked. Keep digging until you receive clear and satisfactory answers. Then make a decision based on the facts, and move forward with caution.

Three of Cups

Characters: The Butcher, Baker, and Candlestick Maker
Nursery Rhyme: Rub-a-dub-dub,
Three Men in a Tub

Three of Cups

Description:

Today's world is a fast-paced place. We rush to work. We tend to problems. There's always more to get done than we can possibly do, and as a result, we worry. Because of this, the day's end is often looked forward to. It brings a time to slow down, a cause for celebration, and a reason to have a little fun. Of course, when there's fun to be had, nothing ignites the party spark like getting together with old friends.

Such is the case with the Butcher, the Baker, and the Candlestick Maker. Exhausted from a hard day's work, they deserve some time to kick back, unwind, and have some fun. The old friends hurry off to their favorite party place, shuck their work clothes, and hop into a relaxing tub of bubbles. Stories flow as freely as the ale in their mugs. So do jokes, smiles, and laughter. Before long, all three have forgotten about the days worries and problems. They are enjoying each other's company, and a party is well underway.

Advice:

When the Three of Cups comes to call, put on a happy face and break out the punch bowl. It's time to party, and the Ancients are the hosts! Feel the tingle of celebration in the air. Breathe deeply of its joy, and allow it to permeate your senses. Let it bubble up inside of you until it spills over onto everyone that crosses your path. Smile. Invite friends over, and don't forget the ones you haven't seen for a while. All of them contributed in some way to your success, for they are each connected in the web of your personal life. Now is the time to give them their due, and sharing your happiness is the best way to start.

Got problems? Push them aside, at least for today. You can always tend to them tomorrow. Take a deep breath and relax. You've worked hard to reach your goals, and you've earned the right to a little fun. Be spontaneous. Take your friends to a place that you've always wanted to visit but have never been. Wear something festive. Lighten your step. Laugh, dance, and have a good time. This party is for you!

Two of Cups

Characters: The Owl and the Pussycat
Story: The Owl and the Pussycat

Two of Cups

Description:

Someone once said that love is a many-splendored thing. No truer words were ever spoken, for it crosses all boundaries, soothes all hurts, and fills all emptiness. But as wondrous as that is, falling in love is different. It makes us feel sick and happy all at the same time. It's as if we need that other person to justify the whole of our existence.

So it is with the Owl and the Pussycat. Even though they're an unlikely pair, nothing can stop their hearts from beating as one. Language barriers and cultural diversity make no difference. They are totally devoted to each other and committed to sharing what life has to offer.

Here we see the happy newlyweds sailing off for their honeymoon in a pea-green boat. Quite pleased with the situation, the Pussycat looks at the Owl as if he hangs the Moon. He polishes her ring lovingly before slipping it back on her finger. It is a reminder that no matter what life throws their way, she shall always be the brightness that burns in his heart.

Advice:

When the Two of Cups sails into your spread, it's time to say goodbye to solitary life and start making plans for two. The relationship you've always dreamed of, the one filled with love and commitment, is on the way. And if you're not ready, it may just sweep you off your feet.

While this card frequently pops up in the midst of a serious romantic involvement, it always appears just before a proposal of marriage or the offer of a firm commitment of monogamous love. But what if the two of you seem to have little in common? Then follow the old adage that says "opposites attract," and leave it at that. Truth be told, cultural difference, religious variance, and ethnic diversity don't matter much when it comes to love (neither do likes and dislikes or differing hobbies). Some sort of common ground brought the two of you together; all you have to do is remember what that special thing was, and build upon it.

Don't worry if your friends and family don't totally approve of your choice. Some of the most romantic couples in history were unlikely candidates, yet they managed just fine. Once your loved ones see how happy you are, their approval will come.

Ace of Cups

Depiction: A chalice

Ace of Cups

Description:

The Ace of Cups is, perhaps, one of the most gorgeous card in any Tarot deck. It embodies the splendor and joy of love, the most beautiful things in life. Symbolizing the Moon and its effect on the emotions, the goblet depicted here is cast of silver. Gold, the metal of the Sun, accents the piece. This reminds us that warmth of heart is the first signal that love is afoot.

This loving cup is, however, much more than a mere ticket to romantic joy. Its ribboned bells jingle sweet melodies to the Universe, and announce that we're also ready to accept spiritual love. When we open ourselves up to that, many personal wonders occur. Synchronicity comes into play. We claim self-love and learn to appreciate ourselves unconditionally. And once that happens, a soul mate often appears. Before long, our cup simply overflows with all that is beautiful, harmonious, and joyful. Its waters spill forth, nourishing all in its path and enriching our lives. As a result, we blossom freely, reseeding the love and joy we feel, introducing it into the lives of all those around us.

Advice:

When the Ace of Cups blooms full in your spread, it's time to embrace the power and joy of true love. Allow the swirling mist of romance to envelope you, energize you, and bring forth your inner beauty. Inhale its heady perfume, and let it become an integral part of your existence. Take time to think with your heart instead of your head. Open yourself to new relationship possibilities. Don't worry whether someone is right for you or not. Let Destiny take Her course. True love is right around the corner, and it's waiting just for you.

Allow the joy of love to swell within you. Let it germinate, sprout, and blossom. Embrace its beauty with open arms, and experience the personal transformation that only love can bring. Accept every wondrous gift it has to offer you. Express your emotions openly, freely, and honestly. Follow your heart without worry of what others might think. Don't be overwhelmed by the fullness of your heart. Enhance someone else's life by sharing your heart's overflow. Offer a hug or kiss. Give a compliment. Lend a friendly smile. These are the most precious treasures humankind has to offer—much more precious than silver or gold.

The Suit of Pentacles

Pentacles represent the fertility of the Earth and the riches we gain from it. The soils of our planet are nourishing and fertile. They provide us with food, plant life, and beauty. Earth also brings us the conveniences necessary to live in today's world (wood, metal, glass, paper, and so forth). However, the most important gift it bestows upon us is a secure and solid ground on which to live.

Because the Earth element totally depends upon the other three elements—Air, Water, and Fire—for its existence, the suit of Pentacles draws upon all four for its wealth. Pentacles signify abundance and fruitfulness. They are harbingers of money, success, and luck. They speak of business matters, opportunities, accomplishment, enterprise, and status. A spread comprised of many Pentacles signifies good fortune and often, a financial windfall.

The grapevine borders of the lesser cards of this suit indicate the sweet richness of the life's bounty. They remind us that in order to reap its goodness, we must first carefully till our spiritual soil, sew fertile seeds, and pluck out the weeds of inertia. It's hard work, but the fruits of our labors are well worth the effort.

King of Pentacles

Character: Robin Hood
Story: The Adventures of Robin Hood and His Merry Men

King of Pentacles

Description:

As the King of Pentacles, Robin Hood rules Earthly riches and material goods. Bound to the Earth and its stability, he has an exorbitant amount of wealth. His wealth doesn't just lend itself to financial matters, though. He's also rich emotionally, mentally, and spiritually, and he shares these treasures with all who cross his path. This King is a generous sort who enjoys doing for others, but make no mistake, he's nobody's fool. He expects others to do what they can for themselves, and often restrains his generous nature until he sees whether or not others will put forth any personal effort. If they do, his blessings are many and endless.

Because of his connection with the Earth, the King of Pentacles also has an intense respect for Nature and loves the great outdoors. His ideas always manifest in reality and bear fruit. His reputation for creative thinking and good judgment brings others to him for advice. He's a superb friend and business partner. However, because of his earthy romanticism, he also brings a sense of adventure to every new task.

Advice:

When the King of Pentacles dashes into your spread, take some time to re-evaluate how much you give to others, and how much you save for yourself. Though you see your generosity as a healthy investment in human nature, you may be unnecessarily wearing yourself thin financially, emotionally, and mentally. Instead of doing everything for everybody, learn to fully assess a situation before coming to the rescue. Then offer assistance in direct proportion to the personal effort being made. Remember, also, that money doesn't always fix everything. Often, good ideas, a bit of creative maneuvering, or some sound advice may help much more than extra cash. Understand that if you single-handedly tend to the situations of others on a constant basis, they can never learn to help themselves.

This is also a good time to learn to accept rather than to give. Realize that accepting praise, thanks, and assistance from other people doesn't signal a flaw in your stability. It's often the most generous gift of all. It makes people feel useful. It makes them feel as if they are doing their part. But most of all, it makes people feel good about themselves; and that's a treasure all the money in the world can't buy.

Queen of Pentacles

Character: Maid Marian
Story: The Adventures of Robin Hood
and His Merry Men

Queen of Pentacles

Description:

Maid Marian, the Queen of Pentacles, rules the Earth, its abundance, and all that is fertile in both the spiritual and material worlds. She is a Queen in every sense of the word, for she lacks nothing. She is bright, stable, financially secure, and creative. Though she enjoys living in the lap of luxury, she realizes that true wealth is a matter of personal perception—so much so, in fact, that she manages to find it where ever she goes.

In touch with both her physical and spiritual selves, the Queen of Pentacles is the Earth Mother personified. She nurtures and empowers all who cross her path, never failing to give them the touch of tender loving care that makes them feel that they are uniquely special. She has a great respect for both material and spiritual wealth, and for the fertile bounty of Nature. A well-rounded woman, this Queen knows no bounds. She is just as suited to raising well-adjusted children as to effectively ruling kingdoms, and she gets equal joy from both.

Advice:

When the Queen of Pentacles parades into your spread, it's time to take stock of all you've gained and count your blessings. Remember that there's a silver lining to every cloud; that there is some amount of beauty in everything that touches you. Every moment of your life holds a blessing of sorts. Now is the time to open your eyes, your heart, and your arms to embrace it.

Feel the richness of life reverberate around you. It's in the earth, your friends, your family, and in your life experiences. Make a point to increase your wealth by giving something back today. Take a moment to listen. Use your sense of fair play to solve a problem. Offer some well-thought-out advice. Remember to give a hug. Nurturing others not only empowers them, but empowers you as well.

Take steps to increase your wealth at the workplace, too. Look at the big picture. See the bottom line. Learn to handle situations creatively and for the good of all. Most importantly, help others follow suit. As they learn to work as a team, business will flourish; and as it does, so will the pocketbooks of everyone involved.

Knight of Pentacles

Character: Tom Thumb
Story: Tom Thumb

Knight of Pentacles

Description:

Tom Thumb may be small, but he's certainly not lacking in brains. When King Arthur gave him leave to spend with his family, he offered him all the money he could carry. He could have opted for saddlebags filled with gold dust. That would have made him feel rich. Instead, though, he requested something much more practical. Something he could spend. He only asked for a single gold coin. Not only would the money last throughout his journey, but his trusted mouse could carry it with ease.

Here we see Tom atop his royal steed. He's excited about going home and in a hurry to leave. The armor he wears tells us that he is not only courageous in battle, but is also a shrewd strategist who knows when to take action. However, his treasure, the shiny gold coin bestowed upon him by the King, still twirls gaily on the Round Table. Will he ride off and forget it? Will he swoop down in a gallant show of flamboyance and pick it up? Or will he simply ask one of his colleagues to help him with it?

Advice:

When the Knight of Pentacles rides into your spread, collect your wits and open your eyes. Financial activities are afoot and they need your immediate attention. This is not the time to gamble foolishly. Only well-researched plans will work right now and bring the results you desire.

Take a moment to look at the big picture. Then, carefully check every detail to be certain that what you see is actually what you're getting. If a contract is involved, make sure you read the fine print. If there's something you don't understand, ask questions. Better yet, take the papers to someone well-versed on the issue. He or she will be happy to explain any sketchy clauses to your satisfaction, and render sound advice.

Finally, think about how this financial affair affects you, and what you have to gain. If it looks like you may be on the losing end of the deal, take immediate steps to rectify the problem. Use your head. Open your mouth. Refuse to enter into any agreement that doesn't suit your needs. Remember that there is no situation so bad—financial or otherwise—that can't be turned to your benefit. You just have to take time to think things through.

Page of Pentacles

Depiction: A counting table

Page of Pentacles

Description:

The Page of Pentacles is a fortunate card, for it denotes financial growth and wizardry. And no other depiction could speak its meaning any clearer than the one we see here. It's a counting table; the place where money is collected at the end of the day, where accountants tally and total all incoming funds, and check them against their losses.

The marks on the parchments sheets tell us that this has been an exceptionally profitable day. It's been so busy, in fact, that the accountant is at his wit's end. Worn to a frazzle, he's finally gone in search of help so he can take a much needed and well-deserved break.

Weighed, measured, and tallied stacks of gold coins wait patiently for a place in the safe. A purse spills open, leaving its shimmering gold contents to spill forth across the table. Unmeasured coins lie here and there as they wait for their turn on the scales.

The merchant is so happy, he feels like jumping for joy. There were no losses today. Not so much as a penny. Of course, this means that he, himself, may also have to help with the counting, but he doesn't mind. After today's business, he'll be laughing all the way to the bank.

Advice:

When the Page of Pentacles appears in your spread, it's time to sharpen your pencil and get out the calculator. The Cosmic wizards are smiling on you, and financial deals are headed your way. Now is the time to negotiate all business matters to your best benefit. If something isn't to your liking, ask for changes. Your every request will be granted promptly and efficiently.

If financial matters involve contracts, read them carefully, and don't forget the fine print. Make sure that everything is in order, and that you understand your responsibilities fully. If you're unsure of a particular clause, ask for clarification. Then, sign your name on the dotted line, sit back, and count your money.

This card often brings personal investment opportunities and other money-making offers. Use your head when making related decisions. Examine the figures and look at the profit margins. We seldom get something for nothing, so if it sounds too good to be true, it probably is. Be shrewd. Invest wisely. The money you need will follow.

Ten of Pentacles

Characters: The Prince, Princess, Bird, and Horse
Story: The Golden Bird

Description:

Wealth abounds where these newlyweds live. They own the castle pictured in the background, and the grounds on which it sits. Their apple trees bear golden fruit. Even their animals shimmer with gold. Be that as it may, though, this couple knows that what really matters is their love for each other, the feeling that their hearts beat as one, and the life they make together.

This knowledge didn't just pop up one day out of the clear, blue sky. Its privilege was earned with sweat and hard labor, then paid for with great tribulation. Though the Prince was promised all the gilded possessions we see here as just reward, he suddenly realized that he wasn't all that interested in them. They couldn't bring him happiness. They couldn't help him reach his goals. More to the point, they couldn't help him build the legacy of love that he wished to pass on to his grandchildren. For that, he needed to win the heart of the Princess; for she meant more to him than all the gold in the world.

Advice:

The Ten of Pentacles is a card of legacy, and represents the epitome of family life and its related wealth. Count your blessings and be thankful for all you have. Look past material possessions and monetary value. Real wealth is more than money—it's love given, wisdom gained, and ideas shared. We find it in hugs, in smiles, and in roll-on-the-floor laughter. Real wealth is found in the part of ourselves that we give away freely—the part that expects nothing in return, and lives on long after we do.

If you're currently involved in an intimate relationship, there's a good chance that marriage or long-term commitment propositions may pop up. Follow your heart when giving your answer. The time for steering clear of commitment is over. Know that there is strength in partnership and wealth in promise. There's nothing to fear.

Occasionally, the Ten of Pentacles also signifies a sizable inheritance. If this applies to you, share the money with loved ones. Use it to better their lives. In doing so, you will also better your own life. Remember that what comes around goes around. In this case, sharing your fortune will only add to your total wealth, financial and otherwise.

Nine of Pentacles

Character: A Leprechaun
Story: Tell your child about the pot of gold
at the end of the rainbow.

Description:

Steeped in legend, the rainbow is something that every child looks for after a storm. Sometimes it appears. Sometimes it doesn't. Of course, that makes seeing one all the more special—so much so, in fact, that most children regard its every appearance as a truly magical event.

Ancient folklore corroborates their assumption. It tells us that the rainbow is more than just an array of beautiful colors in the sky. It tells us that the vibrant arch forms a seemingly endless bridge, and that whoever has the tenacity and gumption to track its final destination will be richly rewarded by finding a pot of gold at its end.

Here we find the recipient of such a reward. The leprechaun, dressed in the green of prosperity and the gold of success, is speechless. He can't believe his good fortune. And yet, there it is: a pot spilling over with golden coins. He doesn't worry about the dark clouds looming overhead. He just keeps smiling, for he knows that they will no longer have any effect on him.

Advice:

If you're lucky enough for the Nine of Pentacles to sweep through your spread, kick back, breathe a sigh of relief, and put on a happy face. Your financial worries are over. Everything you've ever dreamed of is possible. In fact, it won't be long before everything you touch seems to turn to gold!

The appearance of the Nine of Pentacles provides a good time to set plans in motion. The money will be there. It's not a good time to be cocky, however. Though it's quite possible that tons of cash and financial glory may rain down upon you in a single large sum, more than likely it will come in dabs and dribbles. For this reason, it's a good idea to carry out plans one step at a time, and move forward as your ideas begin to bear fruit.

Understand that there are certain cosmic responsibilities that come with financial security and material success. In short, it's now up to you to help tend to those who are less fortunate. As your finances grow, remember to do something nice for someone else. Feed a homeless person. Buy a toy for an impoverished child. Use some of your newfound success to put smiles on other faces, and your pot of gold will never run dry.

Eight of Pentacles

Character: The Sorcerer's Apprentice
Story: The Sorcerer's Apprentice

Description:

The Sorcerer's Apprentice was an ambitious sort. He certainly had more in mind than being a mere assistant when he signed on for the job. What he really wanted was all the knowledge that the wizard held. More to the point, he wanted to be the most powerful sorcerer in the world. The wizard, however, had other things in mind. That being the case, the Apprentice became more determined than ever. He worked up a new plan of action, and carefully set it in motion.

In this depiction, we see the Apprentice voraciously studying spells while his master is asleep. An insatiable student, he thirstily soaks up every magical tidbit. Some of it comes easily to him, and some of it doesn't; but he continues to study deep into the night until he understands each spell in its entirety. Then he memorizes each one, and retains it for future use. Sometimes, he even takes the liberty of practical application, but he always keeps a watchful eye on the laboratory door. He knows the wizard could wake up at any time.

Advice:

When the Eight of Pentacles appears in your spread, it's time to take stock of your job-related skills and employment opportunities. Will the skills you possess really put you on the road to financial security? Will they give you the life you want to live? Even allow you a comfortable existence? If the answer to any of these questions is "No!", the time has come to re-think your current situation, and make some serious changes.

Give some thought to the sort of work you'd really like to do. Don't worry about the reactions of your friends or peers. Their opinions really don't matter. All that matters in this situation is your happiness. Remember that you spend most of your waking hours at work. It stands to reason that the way you make a living should enrich your life and bring you a certain amount of joy.

Once you've decided what you want to do, don't delay any further. Follow through by taking the appropriate steps. Pick up the phone and make a few calls. Enroll in classes. The sooner you are enrolled, the sooner you'll have new skills at your fingertips—skills just waiting to make you comfortable and financially secure. But most of all, they will be skills to ensure your happiness for many years to come.

Seven of Pentacles

Characters: Mary and her garden
Nursery Rhyme: Mary, Mary, Quite Contrary

Description:

If everyone tended the gardens of life as creatively as Mary, their personal problems and obstacles might become things of the past. She paid no heed when the townsfolk said her garden wouldn't grow. She paid no attention when they laughed, pointed, and labeled her contrary. She just went on, tilling the ground and planting her seeds. Mary knew the one thing that they did not: if she wanted it badly enough, her garden would not only grow—but blossom and bear fruit.

Here we see that Mary has, indeed, gotten the last laugh on the townsfolk. We watch as she lovingly tends her garden and nourishes the fruits of her labor. Roses bloom in splendor along the fence. Mary is quite the horticultural magician. She has somehow managed to grow shimmering silver bells, and if we listen closely, we can hear their tinkling laughter carried on the summer breeze. The sunflowers that she calls her "pretty maids" look on. They chat amongst themselves, patiently awaiting a drink from the sorceress who gave them life.

Advice:

Should the Seven of Pentacles ripen in your spread, get out the sickle and basket. Your garden is laden with fruit, and it's time to bring in the harvest—your own financial harvest developed from the fruits of your labor. Whether the bounty is worth picking or not is up to you. If you've sown the seeds of creativity, individuality, and hard work, your harvest will be well worth the wait. If not, chances are you'll find it lacking. Just like the old adage says, you'll reap precisely what you've sown.

If your garden bursts forth with sweet, rich abundance, use the money wisely. Pay off some bills. Make necessary repairs. Apply it to a project that's close to your heart. Remember that you receive in proportion to what you give. If you have any cash left, use it to help someone else in need. It will return to you nine-fold, re-seeding your garden and preparing it for the next successful season.

However, if the harvest was not what you'd expected, take some time to re-think your financial strategies. Determine where you went wrong, and firmly resolve not to make the same mistakes again. Only then will your garden blossom and flourish to your satisfaction.

Six of Pentacles

Characters: The Elves, the Cobbler and his Wife
Story: The Cobbler and the Elves

Description:

When the tired old Cobbler stumbled into bed late one dreary night, he had no idea that the Universe would finally cast a smile his way. He and his wife had worked long and hard for many years just to scrape by. It wasn't that business was bad, there was just too much to keep up with, and the Cobbler couldn't afford a hired hand. Then, one night, the elves came to visit, and left the Cobbler and his wife a wonderful surprise. It was a surprise that would forever change their lives.

In this depiction, we see the elves dancing with wild abandon on the table top. What is the source of their glee? Their brand new outfits, of course! Wanting to repay the elves, the Cobbler worked tirelessly to craft new pairs of boots for both of them. The Cobbler's wife got busy, too. She knew they couldn't possibly wear new boots with old clothes, so she quickly stitched up two new suits from the brightest colors she could find. We can tell by the smiles on the elves' faces that the mode of payment is more than merely acceptable. Obviously, it's a perfect fit.

Advice:

When the Six of Pentacles dances into your spread, remember that one good turn deserves another. In this case, someone who helped you in the past needs assistance. Now it's up to you to give something back.

Spend a few moments thinking about how that person helped you, the difference it made in your life, and what it meant to you personally. Then look at the big picture. Evaluate their circumstances, and determine how you can best assist them. Understand that "assistance" is the keyword here. It is not up to you to resolve the whole of their problems, or fix the situation indefinitely. Because this falls under repayment of Karmic debt, it is only up to you to help them get back on their feet. Leave the rest to them.

For this reason, give only what is needed—what is necessary to justly balance the Karmic scales. Most of the time, this has little to do with what we think is necessary. For by our very nature, we are overly generous when it comes to returning favors. This doesn't mean that stinginess is in order. The best way to assist people is to show them how to help themselves. They may only need a good old-fashioned jump start.

Five of Pentacles

Characters: The Baby Swan and the Ducklings
Story: The Ugly Duckling

Five of Pentacles

Description:

When the Ugly Duckling finally pecked his way out of the confines of the egg, he could hardly wait for the adventures that his new life would bring. It wasn't long, however, before he realized that something was awry. He didn't look like anyone else in the nest. He didn't sound like anyone else in the nest. Even worse, all of his nest mates saw it, too, and they never missed a chance to remind him of it.

Here we see the all the little ducklings swimming in the pond. They glide through the water, playing a game called "outcast." They carefully close their swimming ring to exclude the Ugly Duckling. If that's not bad enough, they fling nasty remarks his way. The object of the game, of course, is to see who can hurt his feelings the most irreparably, and it looks like several of them are tied for first place.

All is not lost for the Ugly Duckling, however. A pair of swans swims gracefully in the background. Will he see them and swim their way? Or will he just continue to be the object of ridicule?

Advice:

If the Five of Pentacles brings its darkness to your spread, you probably aren't feeling too good about yourself or about life in general. Chances are that everything you've held near and dear (home, family, friendships, spirituality) seems to be falling apart. Your physical and emotional health may also be failing. Life as you know it has suddenly ceased to exist, and you don't have a clue how to get things back on track.

First, take steps to fight off any depression looming overhead. Talk to a friend. Join a support group. Swallow your pride and ask for help. Even perfect strangers will help, if they know you're in need. If the crux of the problem is financial, get to work. Take a second job or ask for overtime hours. Understand that this situation—no matter how bad it seems—will pass with time, and that the light at the end of the tunnel will guide you through.

Then do whatever it takes to heal your emotional wounds. Know that you are a special person, and that the Ancients do watch over you. Understand that obstacles in your path are often necessary so that you are able to become who you were meant to be—that strong, resilient person who appreciates life, but can handle whatever it throws your way.

Four of Pentacles

Characters: The Dog and his shadow
Fable: The Dog and His Shadow

Four of Pentacles

Description:

Life is not always what it appears. There are countless mirages and temptations along the way. Couple that with the attitude that "whoever has the most toys wins," and we often come out the loser.

Such was the case with the Dog and his shadow. He'd found a bone on his morning exploration, and was very pleased with himself. It was, after all, quite a specimen. He proudly pranced toward home. As he made his way across the bridge, though, something caught his eye. It was a larger dog with a much larger bone. First, he whined out a plea for a trade of prizes. There was no response. Then, he tried to stare the other animal down. When that didn't work, he let out a low growl. Finally, the greedy dog just reached out to grab the larger bone.

Of course, it never occurred to him that the other dog was simply an illusion, and that what he saw was only his own reflection in the water. Had he realized that at the onset, he might have had a prize to show his neighborhood buddies. Instead, he had nothing to show for his morning travels.

Advice:

When the Four of Pentacles drops into your spread, it's probably an indication that you've become a "pack rat" of sorts, on both the mundane and emotional levels. A creature of habit, you're afraid to let go of anything. You just keep hoarding things away and storing them up because you think you might need them later.

While there's nothing wrong with being prepared, the time has come to simplify. If you haven't used something within the past year, get rid of it. Toss out anything broken as well. The same goes for dysfunctional relationships. Even though these are bad for us, we often stay from force of habit. A new day has dawned, and it's time to turn over a new leaf.

Sometimes the appearance of this card also indicates a selfish, greedy nature. If this applies to you, learn to share and be a little more generous. Understand that real wealth comes not to those who keep everything for themselves, but to those who understand the Karmic Laws. In short, anything you do will come back to you three times three. With that in mind, give freely to all in need. In sharing your good fortune, you will reap more benefit than you can imagine.

Three of Pentacles

Character: Rumplestiltskin
Story: Rumplestiltskin

Three of Pentacles

Description:

When the miller boasted to the King about his daughter's cleverness, he was just trying to impress him. Because the king was as greedy as the miller was proud, they struck a bargain. If the daughter could spin the straw into gold, she would be queen. If not, she would be put to death. It never occurred to the miller that the King might actually put her to the test. Now, because of his bravado, it looked like his daughter might die, and he could not save her. She had no idea how to spin straw into gold. And no one else did, either. What the King had ordered was an absolute impossibility, and the poor miller only had himself to blame.

Rumplestiltskin, however, knew exactly how to please the King. After all, spinning straw into gold was his specialty. Here we see him working at the wheel, happily using his inherent talents and creativity to get what he wants. He's definitely making progress, for we can already see several gold bars tossed into the basket at his feet. But will he be able to spin all the straw into gold before morning? Does he think the bargain he struck with the miller's daughter is important enough to guarantee success? Only the rising of the Sun will tell.

Advice:

Should the Three of Pentacles glow brightly in your spread, take it as a sign to rekindle the fires of inspiration and artistic expression within yourself. You have the ability to make them work towards your financial goals. They've just been sitting on the back burner so long that you've almost forgotten about them.

Spend some time thinking about the talents given to you at birth. They may involve language skills, the ability to draw or paint, a knack at woodworking, or some other creative form of expression. Understand that these gifts weren't just bestowed upon you at the whim of the Ancients. They were given to you to help you get along in this life, and to ease the pains of financial support. To allow them to sit lifeless and unused is tantamount to telling the Universe that Its gifts aren't good enough—that you'd rather struggle needlessly than make use of what you have.

Don't slap the Ancients in the face! Decide how you can turn your talents into extra cash, then get started today. Create a plan of action. Make a few phone calls. Once you show the Ancients that you're willing to work, you'll be amazed at the results!

Two of Pentacles

Characters: Mr. & Mrs. Jack Sprat
Nursery Rhyme: Jack Sprat

Description:

Jack Sprat and his wife are a very unlikely, but happy, pair. He doesn't care that she's just a bit chubby. He sees it as part of her feminine charm. She doesn't mind that he's tall and lanky. In fact, she finds it very attractive. The Sprats are a match made in Heaven. They are just right for each other, and side by side, they strike the perfect balance.

Here we see the Sprats sitting down for dinner, and each has very different items on which to dine. He likes vegetables, but her tastes are a bit richer. However, these sorts of differences do not present a problem. In fact, it's because of them that the Sprats are such a happy couple. They have based their marriage on common ground that is based on the old adage "waste not, want not." Because they have different likes and dislikes, they know one thing for certain. Nothing will ever go to waste in their home or in their lives. More importantly, nothing will ever go to waste in their love for each other, and that's what really matters to them.

Advice:

When the Two of Pentacles appears in your spread, it's time to balance the budget. Get out the ledger and take a long, hard look at how you're spending your money. Chances are that you don't have enough to go around, and have no clue as to why.

Start by looking at your monthly expenditures. Then trim away any fat. This may involve eliminating eating out, movie rentals, magazine subscriptions, and other personal treats. If you don't need it to survive, put the purchase aside for now. Determine the cost of the bare necessities, then work with that figure. Don't spend anything more. It won't be long before your financial problems disappear and money begins to flow freely again.

Sometimes, this card also denotes needless waste. Understand that every penny you earn and everything you buy with it is, in some way, a gift from the Cosmos. To toss it away carelessly is not just bad business, it's downright ungrateful. With that in mind, take a look at what you're throwing away, and find a use for it. Recycle paper, glass, and aluminum. Have a yard sale and turn unwanted items into cash. Better yet, give your surplus to a favorite charity. They'll appreciate it, and so will the Cosmos!

Ace of Pentacles

Depiction: A golden pentacle

Description:

The Ace of Pentacles is the embodiment of the richness of the Earth and all that it entails—fertility, abundance, prosperity, and financial wealth. For this reason, the pentacle is formed of shimmering, shining gold (the metal of the Sun), and it speaks of its riches whenever we glance its way. The center of the pentacle is marked with the phases of the Moon, an indication that a certain amount of balance is necessary to keep Earthly wealth flowing in an uninterrupted stream.

This card is, however, more than just a depiction of a golden pentacle. It is fertile ground to be tilled and planted. Grapevines grow and wrap around its structure, bearing rich, ripened fruit. This reminds us that we are the gardeners of our personal financial status, and that the paths we choose are much like the twirling tendrils of the vine. In short, it is up to us to cling to and claim the riches that await.

The Cosmos, however, has a stake in our wealth as well. It ties the fate we choose in the rich, purple ribbons of power, and adds a few coins for good measure. Because of this, we know that no matter how we choose or how we proceed, a certain amount of luck and good fortune will always be on our side.

Advice:

When the Ace of Pentacles lands in your spread, get out your calculator and call your banker. Money is coming your way, and there's nothing meager about it. Substantial success and power are on the way, too. The Ancients have chosen you as Their payee. And since they have an unlimited checking account, today is your lucky day!

Remember, though, that the Ancients only help those who help themselves. That being the case, do what you can to embrace their offer and ensure your prosperity. Take a chance. Invest in a good cause, or make a small donation to your favorite charity. Know that what comes around goes around, and that your generosity will not only be rewarded nine-fold, but with interest.

Since you are currently on the receiving end of Earthly riches and power, this is also a good time to take a chance on yourself. But what if you don't have a lot of money just now? Then secure your coming windfall with a minimal investment. Buy a lottery ticket. Make plans for a new business venture. Doing so will alert the Ancients that you are ready and willing to accept Their gift and all it has to offer.

About the Author

Dorothy Morrison is a Third Degree High Priestess of the Georgian Tradition. An avid practitioner of the Ancient Arts for more than twenty years, she founded the Coven of the Crystal Garden in 1986, and spent many years teaching the Craft to students worldwide.

Dorothy is the creator of The Whimsical Tarot (U.S. Games Systems, Inc.) and the award-winning author of *Magical Needlework*, *Everyday Magic*, *In Praise of the Crone*, *Yule: A Celebration of Light and Warmth*, *The Craft*, *The Craft Companion*, *Enchantments of the Heart*, and *Bud, Blossom & Leaf*. These efforts have lead to countless media interviews, lectures, workshops, and book signings throughout the United States and Canada.

Dorothy currently lives in Maryland with her husband, Mark, and their black labrador retriever, Sadie Mae.

Bibliography

Andersen, Hans Christian, *Hans Christian Andersen Fairy Tales*. London, England: Paul Hamlyn, Westbook House, Fulham Broadway, by arrangement with Golden Pleasure Books Ltd., 1959.

Clarson, Laura G., *Tarot Unveiled: The Method To Its Magic*. Stamford, CT: U.S. Games Systems, Inc., 1984.

Lesser, Rika; *Hansel and Gretel*. New York, NY: Dodd, Mead & Company, 1984.

Mayer, Marianna; *Beauty and the Beast*. New York, NY: Four Winds Press, a division of Scholastic Magazines, Inc., 1978.

Moorsom, Sasha; *Perrault's Fairy Tales*. Garden City, New York: Sash Young, Doubleday and Company, Inc., 1972.

Opie, Iona and Peter, eds. *The Oxford Book of Children's Verse*. New York, Oxford: Oxford University Press, 1973.

Tudor, Tasha; *Tasha Tudor Book of Fairy Tales*. Bronx, NY: The Platt and Munk Co., Inc., 1961, 1965, 1969.

l
(